MW00625911

Have You Seen My Mother

Bryan Lee
McGlothin

Foreword by
Jerry Bergman, Ph.D.

Taurleo Publishing

This book is dedicated to my mother.
She fought so hard and lost so much. I love you, Mom, and I'll never leave you again.

Acknowledgements

Were it not for the many loving and patient souls surrounding me, lovingly guiding me, I would assuredly still be wandering in the dark. And it is these wonderful family and friends to whom I give thanks for being there when no others were.

No one person has been more selfless than my amazing wife, Evelyne. Her torch of faith for me, many times, shone bright when mine was mere smoke. Her elegant beauty continually turns many a head, yet her inner beauty is a thousand times more brilliant. Without her, I am nothing. Together we are amazing.

Many times my wounds have been tended by my stepsisters, Carrie and Kathy. Having them in my life since the age of three, I feel they truly are my sisters.

My uncle, Walter Ray, and my Aunt Ruth, have taught me the meaning of true love of family. My warmest childhood memories are in their home. I also give many thanks to their daughters, Jackie and Vicky, who supported me in discovering my past.

Jerry and Cindy Gomez' love and support through the years is testament to their enduring affection for family and friends.

The wisdom imparted to me by my dear friend Chris Barrett has helped me weather many a storm. His kindness comes straight from his affectionate heart.

The vivacious Theresa Behenna and her captivating musical talents have often lifted my spirits when my soul was heavy.

The gracious Marilyn and Michael Smith warm our hearts with their abundant love for friend and family.

With her no-nonsense attitude and her Southern Belle beauty, Mary Heafner has always been there in times of need to put a smile on my face.

I always think of Safari and of the special warmth of Joyce and Jack Frassanito's friendship, at the water's edge in the golden sunset.

Thanks also to my long lost, though newfound family: Bryan Mason, Sherry Curry, Vera Wallis and Judy Whitmire. Lola, Sherry and Eddie Franco; and Georgina, Cathy, Coline.

Words cannot possibly express my thanks to Jack Stamper for being at my mother's side for more than three decades.

Many thanks also to Chris and Nina, who introduced me and Evelyne to our wonderful editor and designer, Margaret Burton Malone. Not only was Margaret wonderful to work with, but she has done an amazing job to help bring mine and my mother's story to life.

Author's Note

The dates and locations I mention throughout this book are unchanged. A few (very few) of the characters have fictitious names to protect privacy and relationships. Although some of the dialog was spoken as much as thirty years ago, almost all of the spoken words are very significant and even life-changing, therefore I can say with certainty that I have preserved them word-for-word as often as possible and in the alternative, without distorting the essence of their meaning. I remember them all very well, because I began taking notes concerning the search for my mother many years ago. I am sure that, if there were a way to recall the exact words spoken, they would be so close to the words in the book that there would be no discernible difference between their meanings. Any documents are quoted from original sources or certified copies. The illustrations have been cropped to fit the available space and have been processed to optimize image quality. The only retouching has been to remove obvious blemishes.

Requesting only the truth, my stepsisters Carrie and Kathy have encouraged me in writing my story. I would like to thank them both for their love and support.

Foreword

By Jerry Bergman, Ph.D.

This book is one of the growing body of literature about Jehovah's Witnesses and social problems. It is about the parental abduction of Bryan Lee McGlothin and its destructive after-effects on his entire family. Beginning on the Oklahoma plains in the mid-1960s, the account ends in 2005 with a turn of events that calls for another book. Crafted like a novel, it draws the reader into a harrowing true story of betrayal, kidnapping, drugs, deception, a suicide attempt, and worse. The story stems from a failing marriage, as do many tragic stories, but this marriage dissolved into a 30-year nightmare.

Bryan McGlothin is a talented writer worthy of comparison with some of the best authors. He tells his story with well-paced suspense, contrasted with his quiet faith in the future. The thought-provoking result is a first-rate detective story that keeps the reader looking for clues to demolish lies and reveal truth.

Bryan offers insight into the tragic influence of unbridled religion on mental health. Snatched from his mother in 1966 at the tender age of two, Bryan was denied any contact with her for the rest of his childhood, and only found her after more than thirty years.

Why did Bryan's father—a devout Jehovah's Witness

elder—leave his wife? Angie, a beautiful young Cherokee girl, is pivotal to the story, yet strangely quiet and ethereal until the second half of the book. Why did Bryan's father, Fred McGlothin, kidnap his son and then become a distant, emotionally absent father? Why did Bryan's mother not try to contact her son—or did she?

This compelling story focuses on the Jehovah's Witnesses and how their teachings can lead to criminal and pathological behavior. It offers an inside view of the Witness world that will resonate with Witnesses as well as with non-Witness friends and family: no Christmas, no birthdays, no flag salute, no worldly friends, no college.

Until recently, sexual assault victims who were Witnesses were doctrinally required to prove rape by showing evidence that they resisted with all their strength. Witnesses are still denied full divorce except on grounds of adultery. Rules such as these have consequences that spread deep into the social structure, bringing negative and unanticipated results.

Bryan's personal journey through the Witness way of life shows how, although designed to guide and support the congregation through their problems, an authoritarian religion can create a toxic environment for its faithful. It also throws a searching illumination over the struggles we all face in achieving happiness in this modern age.

Bryan's "dark life" left emotional scars that remain to this day, scars that, even with help from others including a loving wife and several warm friendships, he has not yet been able to erase. The severing of ties to his own daughter—his first-born—under circumstances similar to the loss of his mother indicates that the story will continue long after most of those in this book are no longer with us. It is a story with which millions—Witnesses and non-Witnesses alike—are familiar. Physical abuse, alcoholism, strict religion: these and more are in this journey. The McGlothin story is also about the unconditional love of a mother and son who refuse to give up on their bond: a love that most people seek and never find.

Bryan also shows us how the effects of disfellowshipping (excommunication) go far beyond the obvious and often have unforeseen, tragic, ramifications. Such practices are counter-productive, since they do not help the offender, but rather drive him or her from the religion that practices this form of social control. Every Witness, both active and inactive, should read this insightful work. Above all, this book is a must for every person interested in the long-term tragic effects of parental abduction and the major social problems of today.

Jerry Bergman,
MSBS, MPH, Ph.D. LPCC.

Have You Seen

my
Mother

Introduction

She grows smaller, in the street...

The manicured lawn tickles my feet as the cool, green blades glide between my toes. It is another perfect day in California: warm goose-bumps in the soft breeze. I am very excited: my mommy, my daddy, and I are together again. We spend a good part of the day at Forest Lawn Cemetery, where my maternal grandmother, Lola Mae Mason, is buried. She died nine days after I was born.

My parents are trying to reconcile after swapping me back and forth for two years. My father, born to a farming family, wants to bring his wife and son back to the red sand and clay of his upbringing—McLoud, in the rural plains of Oklahoma. My mother, apparently raised by gypsies, just can't stay in the land of black jack oaks and tornadoes; she wants to travel and see the country. But my father is as hard-headed a McGlothin as any of the men in his family, and he wants to be close to his roots.

My father has made the drive from Oklahoma to meet my mother and me. They met on neutral ground, at the home of a close family friend, Lillie Stamper, before leaving for the cemetery. My mother and Lillie are so close that my mother calls her "Mom."

Earlier that day, she begged my mother not to take me to the cemetery:

1

"Let me keep him with me—"

But Angie would have none of it. "Freddie wouldn't do that," she said.

She's as hard-headed as any McGlothin, and said she could handle the situation. Besides, my father offered her his car keys.

"You can drive," he told her, before placing the keys in her hand. "But I want Bryan Lee to come."

Now, pacing the grass around Lola Mae's grave, my mother stares at her feet, searching for words to make her husband understand her fear of the lonely, confined existence awaiting her on the prairie. Back and forth they argue: each with reasoning the other cannot comprehend. My main objective is to catch an elusive grasshopper.

My father, softening, finally gives in. He'll consider moving to Southern California if she'll seriously try to be a better wife.

She cautiously agrees and they call me back from the chase. We walk the short way to my father's car and head back to West Covina, where my mother and I live.

On our way back from the cemetery, my father complains of stomach cramps, a recurrent problem he blames on his "nerves." He asks my mother to stop and get medicine for his pains, and like any good wife, she does.

She stops at a convenience store, not even one block from Lillie's home, believing that she's in safe territory. She steps out of the car as my father grasps his stomach, wincing.

She enters the store and quickly locates the medicine. As the door swishes behind her, he grabs his spare keys, jumps over the console, and backs out of the parking lot.

The bottle smashes and pink oozes across the floor as my mother sprints for the door. Smoke fills the street as the tires spin, then grip. The car screeches away.

My mother pursues the car on foot, screaming my name: "Bryan Lee! Bryan Lee—"

I stand in the back seat, crying, reaching toward the back window as her arms stretch out; daring me to leap from the car, telling me she'd catch me. She grows smaller in the street as we speed away. A block down the road, we fly around the corner and vanish.

My mother stands in the middle of the street. Her arms fall like dead weights at her side.

Her mind screams: *What did I do?*

I am only two years old, and I will not see my mother, nor hear her voice again, for over thirty years.

Chapter 1

You know Jo isn't your momma, don't you?

At eight years of age, I heard this story for the first time, from my own father. It was a weekend and we were watching football; my stepsisters, were away.

I lay on the floor; my father sprawled on the sofa. As the game wound down, he asked a very simple, yet odd, question:

"You know Jo isn't your momma, don't you?"

"Yeah," I replied.

Although it was something I never talked about, I knew by then that Ina Jo, my father's wife, was not my mother. I'm sure the subject was brought up from time to time while I played with my stepsisters, Kathy and Carrie.

What is this all about? I wondered. *This has got to be something really big!* I had never thought of my mother's actual identity until then; I was not supposed to speak of her. I was transfixed.

I could not know that this conversation was just one step on an unbelievable journey, one that had already lasted almost a decade. The family whispers fell silent when I was present, so I was unaware of what I had already been through.

"Well, your momma's name was Angie," my father said as I settled in for the story. "She was a very pretty woman with long black hair and a real light complexion."

My mind raced as he spun his tale of a woman I never

knew. I couldn't believe it! Yesterday I was nobody, but today at eight years old, I had a mother! And her name is Angie, and she was pretty. *What happened to her?* I wondered.

"We had some good times and bad," he said, explaining that she did not come from much of a family. They lived a gypsy life. Her father, my grandfather, was drunk much of the time. In fact, my father later said that, when he married my mother, my grandfather was drunk at the wedding.

"She was disfellowshipped," he continued, spinning his story. "We got a divorce when you were about three, and then I married Jo."

My fascination immediately turned to distress. Being raised as a Jehovah's Witness, I knew being disfellowshipped was ominous. She had to be very bad indeed to be excommunicated from the Organization.

"Do you have any pictures of her?" I asked.

"No," He replied. "I had some letters and stuff of hers, but we threw it all out."

"Why?" I asked. *I need that stuff,* I thought.

"Well, we thought she might be demonized."

I was silent as my heart tumbled to my stomach: *Here I am, only a kid; I just learned I have a mother, her name is Angie, and she's demonized.*

At that moment I new I would never see my mother. I knew what it meant to be demonized, and it scared me. We studied this in the Kingdom Hall all the time, but never in my wildest dreams did I think of my own mother possessed by the devil.

"She was demonized?" I said, waiting to hear more.

"Yeah, and she liked to party, so we thought it would be better to throw her things away," he confessed.

I didn't know what to think. I remember imagining my

mother dancing, *partying,* in the dead of night to the pounding of the drums: a squawking chicken over her head, blood dripping to her lips. What did all this mean?

My head spun. *My God! If my mother is demonized, what am I?* What I thought was going to be a fantastic tale of intrigue turned out to be my worst nightmare.

My father continued with his story of the day when, in September 1966, he kidnapped me and drove away as my mother ran down the street.

He explained how, from that point forward, he took me on a whirlwind of travel from state to state, town to town, home to home. We were always moving, hiding, running, to keep one step ahead of her. By the time I started the first grade, I had lived in California, Oklahoma, Kentucky, Indiana, Arizona, Arkansas, and Texas.

It was in Kemah, Texas, that we finally rooted ourselves for eight years. But I still find it difficult to live anywhere more than a year.

I felt I was some sort of illegitimate child. *Yes, now I know I have a mother, I know her name, but I dare not tell anyone. She's demonized!*

To a Witness, being demonized is the worst of the worst, for you cannot be more opposed to God than to be one with the very entity that hates Him and all His people. I knew it was over. Just as quickly as I discovered my mother, I had lost her to the unspeakable Evil Forces. I was crushed and knew I would never see her again, *for who would dare seek out the Devil?*

My father, Fred McGlothin, was born in April 1938, near Oklahoma City. He was raised in McLoud, Oklahoma. He was the second son of Buck and Lucille, and brother to Walter Ray, Jessie, and Everett, the late comer. The McGlothins were a poor but proud family, who worked at odd jobs as well as farming and selling vegetables on the roadside. In fact, my father failed first grade because he missed so much school to work in the fields. Those were tough times and everyone did their part; no-one more so than my grandmother Lucille, a tiny woman who gave birth to twelve-pound boys.

I have only a few memories of my grandmother and Uncle Everett. In one, my grandmother wraps her arms around me as I sit in her lap and listen to the old people, talking about old people stuff, in their small country house. I'm about four years old.

In another, my Uncle Everett, a bit of a goose, is outside playing in the hot sun. He tells me to grab a watermelon and run. I pull the heavy, cut half-melon down from the roadside vegetable stand in the front yard and follow as fast as my little legs will take me. We catch up with my cousin Dennis—he is my age—just as he is easing through the barbed wire fence, heading home. Everett scoops handfuls of melon and pelts Dennis with the sticky fruit. I jump into the fun, wielding seed-laden, soggy projectiles of oh-so-sweet watermelon.

Dennis was none too happy with us; I'm sure he needed a bath once home.

My uncle Everett was only about eight years older than me and I suppose it showed in his childish ways. Those are, sadly, the only two memories I have of my father's mother and youngest brother; both died early.

In 1970, during intermission as we ate from our fruit bags at a Jehovah's Witness Convention in Corpus Christi, Texas, we heard my father's name called over the echoing loud-speakers. He was visibly upset when he returned. He had been informed that his mother and brother were killed by a drunk driver while out preaching.

My father and stepmother left immediately for the funeral in McLoud. My stepsisters and I stayed with friends in Corpus to weather out hurricane Celia, which hit a few days later. From that day forward, at any Jehovah's Witness Convention, if someone's name was called over the loudspeakers, my father always lamented, and felt sure someone was soon to hear of a fallen loved one.

My grandfather was strong as an ox and just as stubborn. He carried great pride and saw things in black and white; his sons did not fall far from the tree. As big and stern as he was, he always loved the children and had a story and a piece of candy for each of them.

"You know why everyone calls me Buck?" He asked once.

"No," I replied.

"My friends call me Buck, because even if they're flat broke, they still got one *Buck…*"

I enjoyed being with him and listening to his tales of hunting and fishing. He once bragged that one winter, the family had nothing to eat. Having no bullets for the rifle, he set out to hunt rabbit with his claw hammer. The snow was so deep, he said, that the rabbit could barely move forward for having to jump so high to get out of the bottomless snow. He said they ate heartily that night, thanks to his trusty claw hammer.

His stubbornness caused controversy at times, as it did when he grumbled that the book, *Your Youth—Getting the Best Out of It*, printed by the Watchtower Bible and Tract Society, stated that masturbation was against Biblical principles, even stating that "In fact, masturbation can lead into homosexuality."

"The Society aught not to print stuff like that!" He told

me. His contempt was not because the Watchtower was trying to link masturbation to homosexuality. He couldn't believe they would print something of such a personal nature. I was amused because I knew if he had voiced his displeasure to any other Witness, he would have invited trouble. It's not a good idea to speak out against the Watchtower.

Sadly, Buck died in 1990, from heart failure.

My father and his family hardly ventured out of the Lincoln County area of Oklahoma. He graduated in 1957, from McLoud High School: one of a class of thirty-four.

His favorite sports figures were Kenneth Holder and Billy Joe Fisher and his favorite band was "Ferlin Husky and His Hush Puppies." Ironically, in 1956, Ferlin Husky released a song titled "Sinful Secret."

My father grew up in the new age of radio and TV. In his youth, he listened to crackly AM broadcasts in their small home; a TV was too costly. He was intrigued by the new industry of electronics, which became his passion. Several schoolmates wrote in his graduation booklet, calling him an "electronic brain." Bus McVay, the class President, wrote: "Freddie, You'll make a great scientist someday. Good Luck." He pursued his passion by working as a TV technician in McLoud for F. P. "Shine" Rhodes, at the Rhodes Furniture and Appliance store.

Although his family seemed content there in the farming community of McLoud, my father dreamed of going places, having nice things, and of getting away from the red dirt of central Oklahoma.

He was looking to trade his moonshine for MacAllan and wanted more from life than what the farm had to offer. While his parents and brothers were pleased with the windswept dirt roads, he was bored. Traveling to out-of-the ordinary places was one of his first discoveries. His favorite destination was Mexico.

My Aunt Ruth, Walter Ray's wife, still tells the story of my father returning from Mexico and bringing them "guacamole."

"It looked like baby shit." Ruth recalled. "Sat in the icebox till it turned moldy, then it got throw'd out," she laughed.

My father was raised a Jehovah's Witness by his father. He became a servant in the Organization in his early twenties. By his late twenties, he was giving hour-long sermons to the congregation. He seemed a pillar to the Witnesses around him and a real catch to many a Witness girl.

As a young man, he enjoyed his independence and did not marry until twenty-four years of age. He married Angie Lenora Mason, my mother, who was nine years his junior.

Angie was born in Tucson, Arizona, in March 1947, the daughter of Lola Mae Turner and Bryan D. Mason. She was raised a Jehovah's Witness by her mother. For years, all I knew of my mother is what my father told me that fateful day. She was the woman who carried me for nine months and yet she was an enigma. My father trained me to fear her, but thanks to my natural instincts, I also longed for the woman I never knew.

As a young boy, a few of my father's family teased me with anecdotal stories of my mother, but the fear of my father discovering my curiosity kept me from pursuing any drawn-out conversations concerning her, so I kept quiet.

Through the years my father repeated to me how she ruined his nerves by disappearing with me, leaving him clueless as to my whereabouts. His grimace as he told of countless amounts of money spent on lawyers, plane tickets and road travel to California to rescue me revealed his disdain for her;

she had taken a toll on his health and wallet as a young man, he said.

My father eventually grew lonely, he said, and the burden of raising a two-year-old alone while working full-time was became overwhelming. He knew his divorce from my mother would soon be finalized and eagerly awaited his new life. I was along for the ride, whether I wanted it or not, without my mother.

Chapter 2

We don't do anything anymore

It was late 1967 and Fred's divorce had just been finalized; my mother didn't bother to show up in court. He had heard just months earlier, through friends, of a divorced mother of two in Duncan, Oklahoma, who was also a Witness. Her name was Ina Jo Williams and they soon began corresponding. For the most part, the totality of their courtship was letters. Jo had been single for some time and as she said, "back then," a divorced Witness woman did not actively seek out a mate. It was frowned upon. Though Fred was not as handsome as Jo was beautiful, no doubt his attention was welcomed. Following a meeting with his family, and a three-month courtship via the United States Postal Service, he and Jo married in December 1967. I was three years old, Carrie five, and Kathy seven.

Melding into one happy family was my father's goal, but the constant moving and hiding from my mother put a strain on the family. My childhood was a dark time. I lived in a house with four other people and yet I was alone.

For years, I had no idea what the emotional impact my abduction had on me as a small child. To be torn from my mother at age two must have left me with emotional scars. The humiliation of bed-wetting plagued me for years, not to mention the constant punishment for the crime. I felt helpless.

It was as if they thought I was too lazy to get out of bed to use the bathroom, but it was out of my control. I continued to wet the bed and they continued to discipline me. One day after school, I arrived home to discover my wet mattress on the front porch. The humiliation is no less for a child than an adult.

I imagine that at three or four years of age, I remembered loving times with my mother just as I did my abduction. And though I recall no difficulties getting along with Carrie and Kathy, other than breaking one of their toys every now and then, I do remember many conflicts and abuses from their mother.

At one time she would gently toss a ball in an underhand pitch while I followed with the strongest swing of my giant plastic bat. Then, running as fast as a new Tonka truck, I would speed around the yard as Jo pretended to chase me to home plate. There in the backyard, in the beginning, we played ball. But my days of play did not last long.

The faded cedar fence soared to the bright blue sky. I don't recall being able to reach the latch, but one way or another, the gate was no obstacle. I was out exploring and at about four years old, it was my first expedition beyond the confines of the backyard. I was absorbed in exploring the neighbor's yard when my left shoulder shot up and I seemed to levitate above the green grass.

"Bryan!" She yelled.

I had no clue what I had done wrong, but I knew I had taken a wrong turn somewhere. Jo whisked me back through the open gate towards our house. My left foot barely skirted the ground at each bounding step as I tried to keep pace with her and her fury.

Yanking me into the house, she swung me into my room. I

expected to be lifted onto the bed and told not to move until my father got home. But this was not even the usual middle-of-the-room spanking. She stopped me just inside and whirled me to face the edge of the half-open door, leaving me opposite the latch. After placing my hands on the door knobs, one on each side of the door, and threatening my life if I let go, she returned as quickly as she exited with a hard leather sandal.

As she scolded me for leaving the yard, she tore down my pants and underwear to my ankles. I never let go of the knobs but my little legs jumped and ran in place as she turned my little white bottom a rosy red, repeating over and over how she had told me not to leave the yard.

I don't remember how long it lasted, but I do remember the pain and the fear.

Perhaps she was frightened because there was a swimming pool next door, or maybe a dog. Maybe she was upset with my father and simply had no patience for me that day. I don't remember the reason, but I do remember the consequences.

I recall being terrified that if I let go the door knob the beating would last longer so I held on tight. I remember the sandal: its hard leather sole with thin, white straps. It had no heel and fit her right hand—and my bottom—to perfection. I didn't leave the yard without permission again.

Jo was a formidable presence in my little world and she enforced her will without oversight. Many times I looked to my father when I felt I was being unjustly condemned. He was almost never there for support; in fact, he was almost never there for me at all.

Though my father fought constantly to "protect me," as he put it, I did not have the relationship with him that my stepsisters, Kathy and Carrie enjoyed. My father and I never had much of a relationship at all: not what you'd expect between a father and his only son. As I grew older, the cold expanse between us became all too evident.

As children, we live moment to moment, taken by the winds of daily life. As we grow older we examine, evaluate, and study not only people and events around us, but also our own lives. In reality, we are the culmination of our past, molded in ways that will affect us until the day we die.

Kathy and Carrie were not difficult to live with, and I remember I enjoyed playing with at least Carrie. But they were the ever-present benchmark from which I could judge my standing in the family. I was dealt with differently from "the girls" as Dad and Jo have always called them. My father would tease my stepsisters, grabbing at their feet while watching TV, play little practical jokes with them.

This is, unfortunately, often the nature of things in blended families. But I always thought it went both ways, with each parent a bit more biased toward his or her own children.

The phone rang late one evening. It was for Kathy: one of her girlfriends. She stepped out the back door for privacy; more than once I caught Jo with her ear to the door jamb, starving for anything audible. In 1975 we had no cordless phones, but we had a very long receiver cord. So Kathy took her conversation outside, along with the kitchen stool. Meanwhile, my father grabbed a poncho and sombrero—souvenirs from Mexico—and sneaked away from the house.

As Kathy continued her conversation, my father emerged from the dark from about fifty yards away, stumbling across the lawn as though he inhaled too much tequila. When Kathy finally realized an old drunk was coming for her, she abandoned her stool and bolted inside, screaming like a little ban-tie rooster that someone was after her. Of course once the door opened and she saw Dad, she hit the roof. Even I had a good laugh at it.

This was the attention I yearned for from my father as I was a child, and that my stepsisters received on a regular basis. It wasn't until my mid-teens that he started showing me any interest. By then it was too late. I felt awkward about his affections. The first thought that would shoot through my mind was: *if Kathy or Carrie were here, you wouldn't even bother with me.*

Even as an adult, I thought it was great that my father did that for them: showing a little extra love and attention. I used to rationalize my father's lack of affection for me. I used to tell my friends that "my father tried so hard to make my stepsisters feel like he was their real father, he forgot about me."

There were times in my childhood when it seemed my father was making genuine efforts. In League City, Texas, he bought fishing gear for us: for me, really. I was about seven years old and was thrilled that my father and I were doing something together. It was the boys' day out.

We left the girls at home and ventured off, father and son. I seldom remember just the two of us doing things, unless it was to deliver a TV too large for him to handle alone.

He parked the white, stripped-down Ford and we walked towards the lake, carrying our poles and a miniscule tackle box. The towering bamboo forest, following the side of the road on the way to Clear Lake, added mystique to our adventure. Though I had never fished, I was ready to reel in the largest in the lake.

Though I have no other recollection of that day, I do remember it as an exciting rarity.

A short time later, we went fishing in Galveston Bay with

a friend and his family in their boat. It was a beautiful, sunny day on the bay and my first time in a boat. I was excited to be fishing where I could never have cast my pole. New to the sport and still quite young, I turned my back on my fishing rod long enough for a fish to hit and take it for a test drive into the bay. I cried. Dad scolded me for my negligence, but then our friend gave me another pole and said not to worry about it.

The few times when it seemed I was really being included in the family, Jo would take the initiative to bring me back to earth. She absolutely wore the pants in the house, which did nothing to help my cause. She was more tough and strict than my father, which left me many times feeling rejected by the entire family.

Members of my father's family often told me I looked just like my mother. I assumed this was the reason why my father treated me with disdain at times. I reminded him of her: the demonized one.

Perhaps if Jo had tried to grow a relationship with me, as my father did her daughters, it wouldn't have been so painful. But that definitely wasn't the case.

Even as late as my twenties, Jo laughed as she recalled the story of *breaking me*—her words—as a young child. After she married my father, when I was probably three or four, I would wake up when he left the house for work. From the age of two, after my father ran off with me in California, I awoke with him; that was my routine. Jo didn't like to get up until later in the morning, so I would sit in the hallway a few feet from her door and wait for her to come out so I could eat.

In Jo's own words, "...so, one morning, he just didn't get to eat. I guarantee you, it broke him of it."

She seemed so proud of herself, to have whipped me into shape. I've heard that story several times through the years, and I suppose what makes it so difficult is that she thinks it's funny. She would never have done it to her own children. But then again, her children didn't need to be "broken."

Often, I would be forced to bed after being punished for some childhood infraction by Jo; I remember lying there and crying to exhaustion. I'd push the air out of my lungs even when there was none, and whisper, "I want my momma!"

Even though she was disfellowshipped and demonized, I thought, surely she'd treat me better than this. Surely she'd have more love for me than I received at this address.

My father had his own TV repair shop in the house in Kemah. Many times I asked him to accompany me to the lake—we lived just a few blocks from Clear Lake—but he always declined. "I have to work," or "I'm just too tired," he would say. I used to think, *how hard is it to sit on a bench and hold a fishing pole?*

I was a lone fisherman for years at the pier on Lake Side Drive. I learned to love it. As a kid, it really didn't have anything to do with catching fish. Though I was overcome with enthusiasm each time I pulled in an unusual redfish or flounder, I rarely caught more than useless hardhead catfish and croakers. The experience, the journey, even the short walk to the pier, was everything to me.

At the pier I was at peace—or I could at least cry in peace. Fishing became my passion because I could spend hours daydreaming; watching the ski boats speed by and counting the wakes as they passed below the pier, one after another. The sailboats would glide over the water like beautiful figure skaters with skirts waving in the breeze. The pier was *my* world, and I was king of the fish and crabs.

With my small backpack filled with peanut butter sandwiches and a mason jar of ice-water, I would head straight to the pier. My backpack was one of my few prized childhood possessions: old army issue, I'm sure, though quite small even for me. My father had given it to me and I used it every trip to the pier. About a year after I received it, it went missing. I searched and searched for my trusty backpack, but had no luck. I asked Jo if she had seen it.

"Yeah, it was in the yard again, so I threw it away." I was devastated.

"It doesn't belong in the yard," she reminded me.

After that day the sandwiches and water went into a paper bag. It just didn't seem the same.

Perhaps I wouldn't have spent the many lonely days at the lake if I had been allowed to associate with the neighborhood kids. "Bad association spoils useful habits" was the explanation I heard more times than I can count as a young Jehovah's Witness.

The last time I played with the *worldly* kids was early on in Kemah. I believe I was in the second or third grade. My father and stepmother told me I would no longer be able to play with any children who did not attend a Kingdom Hall.

"What do I tell them?" I asked.

"You just tell them to talk to me," my stepmother piped. Of course, later that day, Kevin came by. Kevin and I were good friends, and we'd played together for about a year after my family moved to the area. We did the usual kid stuff like climbing trees, riding bikes and playing football; there was no malice in our play. We seldom played at my house, because there was a huge empty lot next to Kevin's. Still, my father and Jo judged all non-Witness children the same; I was forbidden to play with them.

Kevin came by soon afterward, attempting to round up some guys for a game of flag football. I was scared and embarrassed when he shouted my name from the street.

"I can't play with you anymore," I blurted out.

"What?" He said, looking at me as if the holes in my pockets were my invention.

He didn't seem to get it; neither did I, actually. I could feel the heat on my back. I couldn't believe this was happening right in my front yard. I knew I had to get away from Kevin or I'd catch it for sure. As I turned around to get someone to explain to Kevin how evil he was, my stepmother popped out the front door and marched toward us. She was on a mission and I made a beeline to her, knowing her wrath would spike if she thought I was playing with him.

"He wants to know," I told her, as she passed by taking no note of me. She sounded very forceful as she told him I could no longer play with the kids in the neighborhood. She said something about them cursing.

That was the beginning of an even more difficult life for me. Although I was forbidden to play with the kids who lived on my block, I had to attend the same school as they did.

Attending school as a Witness was not easy. The others went on and on about how I thought I was too good for them. The peer pressure was enormous as I was forced to remain apart from the others.

I was coming home from school one day, sitting in the front seat of the bus, talking to the driver, Mrs. Dempsey.

As she stopped in Glenn Cove, I heard "See y'all later, Jehovah!" as I was hit in the back of the head. The guy, probably two years older than me, quickly exited the bus before Mrs. Dempsey could grab him. She did stand up for me, but she was one of the few.

The effect was that it seemed I was putting myself above the other kids, avoiding holiday celebrations as well as the

Flag salute and National Anthem, made my father and Jo's design for my life very difficult to follow. During the Pledge of Allegiance, I would put my right hand over my stomach so the kids behind me would see that my arm was bent toward my heart. As the entire school met in the auditorium for some school affair, I sat on the very back row with a couple of other Witness students. We knew they were going to sing the National Anthem and didn't want the other kids to see us. Unfortunately, the teachers sat behind us all. I felt the whole world breathe down my neck as we three stayed seated and everyone else stood, singing, with their hands over their hearts.

"Are your legs broke or what?!" A tense voice boomed from the coach. Petrified, I turned around and said, "No—" and just then a female teacher gently grabbed his arm as I heard her whisper that we were Witnesses.

Though I had a few friends who tried to understand, being a Jehovah's Witness in school made my world a harsher place.

There was a little relief; our next-door neighbors, the Grays, were also Witnesses. Having them next door was a blessing and a curse. John and Martha's son, David, was two years younger than me and a bit spoiled, but he made a good companion for a lonely soul. We had different interests—he didn't like to fish—but he was someone to play with. He always had cool toys, and his parents did a lot of stuff with him, which was the curse. They often invited me to go to movies or come over for dinner. I could see David's parents did many things with him, and they enjoyed it. His home life was different from mine. I never forgot their attempts to include me in their activities.

I had one true childhood friend. The only problem was that it was a bit of a drive to visit him. Vance and I were like brothers, and even though his mother was a Jehovah's Witness, he suffered severe physical abuse at the hand of his beer-drinking stepfather. Once he pulled out a push broom handle and grabbed Vance by the shirt collar before hauling him away like a hungry lion dragging a gazelle. I fled the kitchen as he dragged Vance to the back porch. Sitting on Vance's bed in Vance's room, I was terrified; his screams wouldn't stop. His mother came in the room, and through her nervous smile told me not to worry. *Why don't you tell Vance that,* I thought. His painful screams continued echoing though the house like the squeals of a pig just before slaughter. I considered trying to get to a phone to call for help, but I was terrified his father would come busting through the door. I contemplated sneaking out the window to get help for my friend. I tiptoed to the casement and tested it. Just then the door flew open. I jumped back to the bed in fear as Vance staggered in and landed on his bed. He lay there crying, red-faced, trying to catch his breath. He was black and purple from his ankles to the middle of his back. Lines of bruised flesh went every which way. Right behind him followed his mother. She sat at the edge of the bed, trying to console him. It seemed so ironic. He was her son, and yet she didn't make the call. Though our abuses were of a different nature, our camaraderie, I believe, was built on our support for one another. He was one of the greatest friends I have ever known. And even though his house was a bit treacherous, I took advantage of any opportunity to visit. I was glad not to be alone.

When my stepsisters were young, we did many things as a family. My father's passion for traveling afforded us several trips to beautiful places like San Antonio, and Colorado, mysterious Mexico and Carlsbad Caverns. Once a year, we traveled to McLoud to visit my father's family. On the way we'd stop in Duncan to visit their relatives and Kathy and Carrie's father, who lived in Comanche.

My stepsisters visited their father quite often when we made our yearly trips to Oklahoma. I remember picking up Carrie and Kathy after their visit with their father during the Christmas holiday. They had so many presents they wouldn't all fit in the trunk with the luggage. Many rode in the back seat with us. One year there was a pretty blond doll and assorted boxes being handed around the back seat, as my sister's gleaming smiles spoke of fun and games around their father's Christmas tree. I looked on with such loneliness and emptiness in my heart. Not only were they receiving wonderful gifts, but they were allowed to visit with their own father. It was so natural and understandable for them to speak about their dad in Oklahoma—*he wasn't Demonized.*

Until we purchased our first station wagon, my seat for the drive was on the floorboard. Once while we drove home after a winter vacation, a beautiful snowfall came and the traffic disappeared. It was very exciting for us kids; we didn't see snow often in the Houston area. Maybe once every five years, heavy enough wet snow would fall to make a dwarfed snowman or a few snowballs; usually, though, I had no-one to receive my sloppy projectiles—or to throw any back.

We continued home at a snail's pace and then, as did other unfortunate motorists that day, my father hit a patch of ice. Half asleep, I could feel the car lean to one side as we slid down the slippery freeway embankment. Being so low in the car, I saw nothing and, by the time I peered out the window, we were surrounded by gorgeous frosty white. I heard Jo tell my father how it was a good thing I was down on the floor. This way I wasn't hurt as we slid into the ditch.

I don't believe my father and stepmother consigned me to the floor for lack of space; I probably weighed no more than a bag of grass clippings. With me on the floor, there was more room for my stepsisters: much as at home, where my bed was in the living room. Our home had three bedrooms and Carrie and Kathy each had their own room. I was used to it.

While we three were young, we had as many outings as most families: a Saturday here or there fishing and playing in the sand on Galveston Beach, bowling with other Witness friends and enjoying movies at the theatre. As my father was an elder, we attended most of the Congregation gatherings, which were a real treat for me. There was no shortage of playmates there and the ballgames were always a welcome treat.

In 1974, my father waited with excited anticipation to see "Lords of Flatbush." He spent much of his time listening to '50s music, so this type of film allowed him to relive a bit of his past, when teenage life was simple: before me and my mother. I was enthralled by the movie. Henry Winkler and Sylvester Stallone with their tough-guy black leather jackets and strong accents on the huge screen seemed so cool. I was ten years old and I wanted to be like them; I wanted some power over my own life. I didn't want to have to take it any more. But it wasn't long before my father and Jo dragged all three of us from the dark time-machine theater. My father, obviously angered, told the manager that the film should have been rated "R."

I learned to lose myself in movies just as I did at the pier. One show with which I truly identified was "The Incredible Hulk." Week after week I sat on the lime-green shag carpet in our living room, which of course matched the curtains. I was greatly enamored with Bill Bixby's character, Dr. David Bruce Banner. All Dr. Banner wanted was to find a cure and be normal again. No matter how strong or clever his efforts, he always ended each show a beaten man. Without fail, the giant green beast reappeared to claim his soul.

I identified with Dr. Brenner because all I desired was to be normal: to be treated as normal and loved in a normal family, not so obviously separated.

On a hot summer day one weekend, while playing in the back yard, I heard the car doors slamming on the station wagon. I sprinted around the garage to the driveway to see who was going where. To my amazement, *everyone* was in the car: everyone but me. It was confusing; I was only about ten years old and I had never known the whole family to leave the house without telling me. But there they were: my father, Jo, Kathy, and Carrie, pulling out the drive.

They had barely moved a few feet when I ran up to the side of the car.

"Where ya'll going?" I asked.

"We're going to see a movie," Jo replied. "We didn't think you'd want to go."

"Yeah, I want to go," I told them.

I felt dejected—and rejected. It wasn't that they couldn't find me; they didn't want to invite me. I'm still curious about what they were thinking. Did they believe I wouldn't care? Perhaps they had no concern how it would affect me. How does a child deal with such insensitivity from his own family? And if they didn't want to include me in the family, why didn't they give me back to my mother?

No matter how hardened I became to living on the outside, the emotional pain was still there in every bone of my body. This was my family, people who were supposed to want me around: to love me. If they didn't love me, then why is that? What did I do?

I was never shown the answers. But I continued my quest to be normal, to get away from the giant green beast.

While Kathy and Carrie were at home, I was entitled to join *most* family activities. Once they became teenagers and no longer wanted to do the *family* thing, preferring to hang out with their friends, family outings came to an abrupt halt.

We no longer did things together. It was as if I was an extension of my stepsisters. If they needed entertainment, then fine, I journeyed along as well. But once they didn't require the attention of our parents, it stopped. The trips, the movies, going out to eat (my father's favorite pastime), all stopped.

Sitting on a tall stool at the kitchen bar one day, I cried as Kathy and Carrie were about to leave to be with their friends.

"Carrie and Kathy get to do everything!" I sobbed.

It was difficult not being included with my sisters; once my father and Jo cut off the family activities, I felt even more alone. Even though I spent many weekends with Vance, my best childhood friend, it wasn't the same. Children want attention from their parents, not to be dropped off to get them out of their hair. They want to be treated fairly within the family. Many a sibling rivalry has been fueled by parents favoring one child over another.

Once Kathy was married, Carrie spent most of her time with her sister, leaving me totally alone at home. By this time the only thing we did on a regular basis was to attend meetings at the Kingdom Hall. Sitting in a chair listening to sermon after sermon is not just deadly boring for a twelve-year-old, it's almost impossible. If I wasn't at a meeting, I was studying for the next one or preaching door-to-door. These became the only family outings for me, but I viewed them as prison time: stuck in the chair at church or stuck in the car driving from neighborhood to neighborhood, knocking on one door after another, praying no-one would be home.

By age thirteen, I'd had it. Even Carrie was having problems at home. I believe she also grew weary of the long sermons and of intruding on people's privacy.

Jo looked like death warmed over one Saturday morning. Her eyes, already red and swollen, filled with tears as she sat on the sofa.

"What's wrong with Mom?" I asked my father.

"Carrie didn't come home last night."

It was obvious Carrie had had enough. Our parents had called hospitals and the police through the night and Carrie was nowhere to be found. The mood in the house was suffocating; I spent my day outdoors. I passed several hours wandering in the woods behind the house, and as I returned home, I saw Carrie's car in the driveway. Curious to hear what had happened to her, I ran to the house and up to the front door.

As I arrived at the door I could hear screaming. Not the high pitch of an argument, but screams of pain. Frightened, I hesitated, and then noticed the curtains were drawn on a beautiful sunny day. The screams continued, and at first I thought I should run away. Then I thought: *What if someone broke into the house? What if someone's hurting my family?*

I made the decision and pushed the door open. I was shocked at Carrie's screams, which filled the room. My feet were glued to the lime-green carpet. Carrie was bent at the hips, my father over her, his stomach to her back and arms wrapped around her, pinning her arms to her sides. Behind her, Jo wielded one of my father's belts. She was whipping the belt back as far as her arm would allow, then with grim determination on her face, bringing it down on Carrie's backside.

Carrie, at fifteen years old, was catching the belt. It wasn't helping her attitude. Her screams now seemed more out of embarrassment and anger as she yelled at both our parents.

My father and Jo both turned to me. I wanted no part of that leather; I'd experienced it too many times. As fast as the door would close, I was out of there. It was the first time I witnessed Carrie or Kathy receiving the same punishment I was used to. It scared the hell out of me. At the same time, seeing Carrie's disdain for authority fueled my contempt for life at home as well, and I rebelled. Slowly, I estranged myself from my father and Jo.

I began sneaking to Kevin's house. His front door faced the street, so I would enter and exit through his window. We would hang out in his room.

In the beginning it wasn't that I wanted to do bad things like drinking, smoking, or drugs. I was just tired of being ignored at home.

Sitting on the floor in the dark room, Kevin and I kicked back one evening and discussed girls and the latest music. When the door swung open, I was terrified. I thought for certain my father had discovered me.

"Oh— Bryan," Kevin's mother said, surprised.

"Hi, Mrs. Smith," I replied, looking up like a beaten dog.

"I didn't see you come in," she casually said.

Even though it wasn't my father, I was petrified. She was an adult and I was certain she was going to report me. Instead, she asked, "Kevin, you and Bryan want a sandwich?"

I couldn't believe it. She was acting as though it was normal to see me there in her son's room uninvited. Obviously Kevin's mother understood; she never told my father I was sneaking into her home through the windows. In fact she was very kind.

As I became more bold and bored, I went from sneaking into Kevin's home during the day to crawling through my own window late at night so I could meet up with other neighborhood kids. That's when I started smoking cigarettes.

I once went with Kevin to some guy's A-frame house in the back of the neighborhood. The guy was lanky and looked a bit dirty, but hey, if Kevin hung with him, it must be safe, I figured.

"Wanna smoke?" Kevin asked.

"Sure," I replied. This was my opportunity to have my first smoke. Finally I was lighting up a cigarette like the cool cats on Lords of Flatbush!

He pulled his pack of Marlboros and cracked one out for me. I wanted to look as cool as possible; I'm sure I seemed anything but. As Kevin was handing me the lighter, I was searching the dark road for signs of my father's truck. I knew if I was caught it would all be over, and life was already bad enough. Though I was aware of the consequences if caught, I took the risk without further hesitation.

"You know how to light it?" Kevin asked.

"Sure," I said, fumbling with the lighter. I somehow managed to get it lit and sucked the smoke into my mouth. *This isn't so bad,* I thought.

"No! Ya gotta inhale it. All the way down," He barked.

"Oh. Okay," I said, and put the cigarette to my lips again.

I pulled hard with my mouth against the filter, and then pulled the smoke into my lungs. Kevin and his friend's laughter broke through the black moist air of the early morning, disrupting the crickets' cadence as I gagged and coughed. My eyes watered as I desperately tried to catch my breath. Kevin was proud of himself for having initiated me so warmly into the world of cool.

While my father and Jo thought the non-Witness neighborhood kids would ruin my wonderful habits, it was Carrie who introduced me to my first high. After she was busted and beaten for staying out all night and not calling, she drew me to her window as I was out in the yard one day.

"What?" I asked.

She held a small brown paper bag out to me.

"I need you to throw this away," She whispered, glancing down both sides of the house.

"What's in it?" I asked, taking the worn paper bag.

"There's a joint in it if you want it. Throw the rest of it away." She shut the window.

After all those years of avoiding the non-Witness kids because of their bad influence, all I had to do to gain my first illegal substance was to cross the hall from my bedroom.

Not long after my stepsister's gift, I picked up another dubie from a kid down the road. Tammy, Vance's sister and Carrie's best friend, was staying over that night and I wanted to impress her and Carrie: to pay back Carrie's gift. I had a tent set up in the back yard and told them when I was all set. Once they arrived in the dead of night, we lit up and passed weed like a three little Indians making peace with the pipe.

I felt part of something! I didn't really know what it was, but it was as if I were truly a part of Carrie's life. It felt great that my older sister wanted to be with me.

Just as we had burnt down about half our smoke and were getting really relaxed, the front flap of the tent flew open. In poked the head of none other than my father.

Every muscle in my body locked up like a tractor trailer screaming towards a heard of cattle. My eyes fixed on his shoes. I knew this was it. I knew my life would never be the same. It felt like getting caught stealing from a blind man. Tammy had just taken a toke and she calmly leaned back on her hands and snuffed out the smoke. Her smoothness revealed her expertise.

"What are you guys doin'?" He said, forcing a smile.

Carrie and Tammy just looked at each other as if they had no clue what he was talking about. He regarded them for an instant, then turned to me and burned holes right through my eyes.

"Smokin'—" I said, in the lowest of voices.

"Smokin' what?"

What could I do? What could I say? The tent was a giant bong and my father had his head stuck in it.

"Pot," I confessed.

"Okay, come in the house. All three of you." His fake smile vanished as he pulled away.

"Please don't tell him I was smoking, Bryan!" Tammy begged me, as though her life depended on me. "I'll do anything!"

I've never had sex with an older woman, I thought. But at thirteen, about to face the firing squad, I didn't take Tammy up on her offer.

The trek from the tent in the back yard to the living room was a death march. Numbness from the pot probably saved me from retreating the other way and running into the woods, taking my chances with *Bigfoot* and the *Creature from the Black Lagoon*. I may have been safer in the black night.

Sitting in the chair, my head bobbed a time or two because my high just wouldn't wear off. Oddly enough, Carrie and Tammy were sent to Carrie's room and were spared the immediate fire and brimstone. My father and Jo's disgust over their little black sheep filled the room as they grilled me.

"What were Carrie and Tammy doing with you in the tent?" they asked.

"Just watching," I lied.

What the hell, I thought. *I'm gonna burn for this anyway, so I might as well make a few points.* I smiled to myself.

Of course this reply was good enough for Jo. Her daughter would never get mixed up in one of my evil schemes. Besides, sitting by the bong is not as bad as sucking on it! To this day I can't believe they fell for that. To my knowledge, neither Carrie nor Tammy was disciplined.

"I don't know what I'm gonna do with you," my father said. I'd heard this one.

Perhaps you could ship me off to my mother was what passed through my hazy mind.

My father, as an elder in the Jehovah's Witness Organization, was a pillar of that community and was thus expected to keep his family within the confines of the Watchtower and *Awake*.

"I guess I'll have to step down as an elder now," He said with revulsion.

They both went on and on about how they did so much for me and how I appreciated nothing. I sat there as usual and said nothing. It was the way I was trained, and I was trained well.

He called John Gray next door, David's father. John was also an elder and asked to speak to me alone, thank God.

"What's the problem, Bryan?" He asked gently.

I couldn't believe someone was asking me if I had a problem. And John was actually sitting there, right in front of me, listening. It was amazing to feel that someone really cared about me. He wanted to hear what I had to say.

"We don't do anything anymore," I said. Then I began to

cry. That was all I could say as I sobbed.

"I know you're a good boy, Bryan."

It was beyond my comprehension that I'd just been busted smoking pot and here an adult was telling me I'm a good kid. It felt so foreign and yet so wonderful and secure.

That is what it had come down to, all the emotional bashing and isolation I endured had culminated in my giving up on the things I considered proper. I felt I had no family: just these two older people ordering me around and forcing me to attend their mind-controlling cult, but no family.

What happened to the father who worked so hard to save his son from the evil mother? Why would he not cherish the days with his child, and relish his accomplishment?

Because of John's visit I was lucky in avoiding the dreaded backroom Judicial Meeting at the Kingdom Hall. It's not a nice experience. My father was not forced to step down as an elder, and I was Privately Reproved.

Private Reproof is much better than Public Reproof. In the latter, the Presiding Overseer elder, from the stage, states that you have been Publicly Reproved, which means those in the congregation can speak to you, but they should think twice about associating with you outside the Kingdom Hall. After this pronouncement of shame, a Special Needs speech is given to inform the congregation what you did wrong. It's humiliating.

It was suggested by the elder body that my father do things, just he and I, to build a relationship (which obviously wasn't there). So, he planned a trip.

Another sun-glossed day in Southeast Texas: my attention seldom turned to my father. With no air conditioning, the wind blasted the cab of the truck, throwing our few words out the windows as violently as the wind had come in. The draft was my only entertainment; I stuck my hand through the window and watched it waft up and down like a Robin's wing on the hot air.

From our home in Kemah, we headed north, just west of the Big Thicket. Before long, smog and shiny buildings turned to towering pine trees and lush bluebonnets. The warm sun and boisterous wind calmed my senses in a vivid blur of dazzling daisies, lively Indian paintbrushes, and fresh-cut grass smelling of watermelon.

Life outside seemed so free and easy compared to the stifling energy in the cab. Still ashamed and embarrassed, I answered my father's queries with as few words as possible and offered none of my own.

We continued up the highway for several hours until we arrived in the old town of Tyler, Texas. Once through the quaint town square, we headed out to the back roads and finally to a secluded trail encased in thorny vines and poison ivy. Deeper and deeper into the Texas jungle we traveled as the branches and thorns scraped the truck-side like icebergs on a ship's hull. I still felt dead inside and kept my eyes on the leaves falling on the dirty white hood.

The tiny trail finally opened to a small clearing; I have no idea how my father found the place. We parked the truck where several others had been as I realized we were surrounded by the backwater slough of a local lake. I was happy to get out of the truck and drop a line into the black water. After all my invitations over so many years, he was finally next to me, there on a quiet bank. Our floats bobbed in the still water and the air filled with the knocks of woodpeckers, the tempo of locusts, and the bass rhythm of bullfrogs. Here I was, finally, fishing with Dad: just father and son. But now it didn't matter. I didn't want to be anywhere with him; I just wanted to crawl into a hole and die. In the back of my mind I knew the only reason he was there with me on that bank was because the elders expected it. He had to make it look as though he was the good father, holding his family upright before God, just as he had for a decade after taking me from my mother; it was all an illusion.

He didn't have time to spend the night. We sat at that slough for about two hours and then made the long drive back home in the still, black night.

Returning home was returning to life as normal; as quickly as our new relationship began, it stopped.

It would be several years before he reached out to me again. By that time, and he and Jo had moved Carrie and I to the East Texas town of Woodville: population 3500. They wanted to save us from the evils of the city and decided the change from city lights to starry nights would be just what we needed as wayward adolescents.

Carrie escaped within months, immediately upon her seventeenth birthday. We soon moved twelve miles south to Warren, where I became used to country living. I traded the calm shimmer of Clear Lake for the gentle flow of Turkey Creek; days of fishing alone on the pier became days of exploring alone in the vast forest.

My days of solitude amongst the Piney Woods of the Big Thicket came to an abrupt halt when we started building our own house. Two years of weekends and one summer were spent on what my father probably thought was quality time: dragging and burning brush and stacking lumber on a slab. If I ever brought up the brass to complain about the lack of child labor laws, I was treated to tales of my father, as a child himself, rising in the morning with snow on his bed. He'd tell how he and his brothers walked a mile in the snow just to get to school.

It seemed a diet of chicken-hawks and possums was in order for my father, as they couldn't afford all the nice things I had the pleasure of enjoying, like a chainsaw instead of an ax.

The move to the country obviously didn't solve our relationship troubles, and my desire to be with my mother was about to slap my father square in the face. Of course, he fought back.

Chapter 3

The popper's kid

Though life at home was more than any child should have to tolerate, there was relief, at least for three summers. Two were while living in the Houston area and one while in Warren after the house construction.

By age twelve, I began spending my summers in McLoud with my father's family. Whose idea it was I can't say, but at the end of one school year my father asked if I'd like to spend the summer with my cousins in Oklahoma. It probably started out as a break for him and Jo. Most likely the summer was too long for her to be around me all day, though she usually made me stay outside during the school break anyway. Regardless, it was a godsend for me.

The second trip almost didn't happen; it wasn't long after I was busted for smoking in the tent. But we had several friends and relatives staying for the yearly Jehovah's Witness District Convention in the Astrodome. There were so many relatives that my Uncle Jessie set up his own tent in our yard.

When I was caught smoking pot, one of my punishments was that I should have no more trips to Oklahoma. Some relatives begged my father to let me return with them for an abbreviated visit. My father relented.

Not only was getting away from my family healing to my soul, but the greatest by-product was that the more time other family members spent around me, they more they were at ease and the more they began to speak about my mother. I learned more about her and the time she shared with my father during those three summers than I had in the past decade. And I was hungry for more.

For my first summer away, I stayed with my Uncle Jessie and Aunt Anna Marie, along with their children: Sandra, Dennis, and Janie.

My father made me spend most of my time there because they were *stronger Witnesses* than Uncle Ray's family. My father was sure I would attend more meetings at the Kingdom Hall and spend more time preaching from door to door if I stayed at Jessie's. I had great times there at my uncle's home, even though there were many rules to adopt. I had other kids to play with, for one thing. We were allowed no TV, except for the news, *Sesame Street*, and *The Electric Company*.

To me, Jessie seemed a miserly tyrant more than a husband and father. Often, we only used one light bulb at night. It was probably only a twenty-watt bulb to boot. Anna Marie would use the bulb in the kitchen while she cooked; the light would barely seep into the living room while we watched the news. Once supper was cooked, Jessie would unscrew the bulb and bring it into the dining room. Through these daily routines of church, Bible study, and conversation, Jessie would spout orders as if he were captain of a pirate ship.

Bible studies were awful. We would sit around the small, circular dining table, like robots, for our Tuesday night Bible study. Perhaps I should say *book* study, since we were actually studying a book published by the Watchtower Bible & Tract Society, not the Bible itself.

We would go through the Witness publication, ask the questions at the bottom of the page, find answers already printed in the book, and mark the publication so that we would be prepared for that night's meeting.

It wasn't so bad, apart from the secret weapon the captain had stowed away under the kitchen table. You never spoke without raising your hand, nor did you laugh, because everyone knew that speaking without permission was met with *the switch*.

Before every study session, Uncle Jessie would make Dennis or Sandra cut a switch from the tree. I don't remember a single study without one of them crying from it. Fortunately for me and Janie, she was very young and I wasn't his child; we didn't meet the stinging wrath of the switch.

Jessie's wife, Anna Marie, was a short, solid woman who kept the kids in homemade desserts and patches on their clothes. With a smile on her face, she kept us all laughing and eating well. She was a wonderful, caring woman who did something unbelievable for me.

When I was twelve and my Father and Jo had come to Oklahoma to pick me up, Aunt Anna Marie told me she had saved some things that belonged to my mother, and that I should ask my father if I could have them.

Oh man, let me tell you. Jessie and Anna Marie lived about a hundred and fifty yards from my grandfather's home where my father and Jo were staying. And if a kid ever flew like the wind, I did that day! I ran through the yard, past the pond, through the barbed wire fence, and landed right in my grandfather's living room.

As my eyes locked with my father's I blurted, "Aunt Anna Marie said she has some of my momma's stuff. Can I have it?" It may have been extremely fortunate that there were several people in the room. He smiled and said yes.

I bolted back down to my aunt's, lighter than any balsa

wood plane I had ever seen. I ran faster than my bicycle had ever dreamed of speeding. As I arrived back at her house, she stood there in the dining area, obviously waiting for me to downshift. She waited there not only as the gatekeeper, but also the keymaster of the knowledge of my entire life. And I had somehow proven myself worthy of entering this new world.

I drew closer to receive the magical reward, and there it was, lying on the table innocently, a spectacular gift from my own past: the other half of me. Upon that old laminated table rested a simple, dusty shoebox and a small roll of woven fabric. I was certain that, upon opening that little box, I would discover my true identity. The box was so small, yet it held the world for me.

"There you go," she said. "I thought you might want these someday." She smiled in a motherly way.

How right she was. I stepped up to the table and pulled the box closer. I gently raised the lid and there they were: two lonely items.

They had probably been in that box for over a decade, and at that moment they breathed new life into my little body. I had never been so close to my mother in my entire life, it seemed. We were connected somehow, the present to the past, by these small objects

I removed a stiff, warped, black-and-white photo. I couldn't believe it. Twelve years old and, for the first time in my memory, I set eyes upon the image of my own mother. There she was, all in white next to my father. It was their wedding picture, taken at the Kingdom Hall in Ada, Oklahoma.

My God—this is my mother! So many years, so many times I had asked my father if he had anything, any small thing I could hold on to, and now I have her picture, I thought.

Surely this woman must have truly loved me.

I stared, and I stared, and I stared. I felt so proud to be her son.

As soon as I could pry her image from my eyes, I returned it to the box and retrieved the next item. It was a small white vase, only about eight inches tall, but still magnificent. It was milky white with semicircular bumps covering its surface.

I held that vase in my hands and studied it closely. My fingers gently traversed the vase, feeling the smooth bumps as a blind man caresses the face of a beautiful woman, imagining with what flower she might have adorned it. It was no less important than meeting my mother for the first time; having that vase in my hands was like getting to know her. This was *her* vase. She picked it out! It was like discovering a small slice of her personality. Did it go in the middle of her dining table, or perhaps on the kitchen counter? Did she fill it with store-bought flowers or fresh-cut ones from the garden? My mind raced with images of her admiring her lovely white vase burgeoning with a rainbow of spring.

I turned my attention to the thick roll of cloth. It was a hand-woven baby blanket: my baby blanket. My father told me it was made by a friend of his after he had spirited me away to Kentucky. My mother probably never saw it.

Needless to say, I was very thankful to my aunt. She was a brilliant star in my life and, I believe, she truly understood the damage my father had done. Aunt Anna Marie was always a warm, sweet woman who obviously cared for me. Unfortunately, she died at only forty-three years old. She will always be part of my warmest memories.

During my second summer in Oklahoma, my great-uncle, Josh, opened my eyes with new information concerning the relationship between my mother and father.

"Your mother was beautiful, and her skin was so sensitive that if the wind was blowin' hard, she'd have red marks where her jet black hair whipped across her face," he remembered. It was amazing to hear someone speak of my mother and, more importantly, to speak well of her.

"Your father was not the best husband in the world," he added.

I sat on the edge of my chair. It seemed impossible someone was actually showing me a glimpse into my parents' past without bagging my mother. My father's own family was imparting to me my first glimpse into the fact that maybe; just maybe, my father shared the blame for their failed marriage.

"Freddie used to spend a lot of time with the boys, and leave your momma home by herself," he explained.

My father wasn't the saint he led me to believe, I thought. He'd always said my mother did this, she did that. His biggest accusation was that she liked to party. And what does that mean? She liked to drink, do drugs—or just wear a clown nose? He was always so vague, but never admitted anything was his fault.

Now an insider, not only an insider, but his own uncle, was spilling the beans. Could it be that my father had not told me the full story? I was fascinated and wanted to know more. I should've known to be careful what I wished for.

My last summer away from home was with my Uncle Ray, my father's brother, and Aunt Ruth. It was the best as far as overall kid fun. There was no daily Bible study or switches under the table. No two-hour meetings to sit through or doors to knock on. All I had to do was be a kid, just me.

They had several children still at home, and that year they lived in the Webber Falls area of Oklahoma. Between the two towns runs the Arkansas River, where we set many a bank pole and caught probably hundreds of catfish.

Vicky was the oldest; by this time, she had already married and I never really got to know her. I spent my days with Jackie, Timmy, Michael, and Carl Dean.

Timmy, in his late teens, was a bit cocky, especially when he got together with his buddy Bruce. Jackie was a little older than Timmy, and she just seemed a kind soul who always listened and was ready to help. Carl Dean and Michael were closer to my age. It was with them I burnt most my summer.

My uncle, Walter Ray, was a man who meant what he said and stood not behind, but next to his word. With his deep voice came authority, but there was a loving heart hiding behind the boom. Aunt Ruth was the mother we all wish we had, and was "Mom" to many kids. She and Ray took in several of us through the years.

"I already got so many kids, one or two more ain't gonna make no difference." She always said.

If ever I experienced true family love, it was in that house.

They were a farming family, one in which everyone worked. In the mornings we'd get up at 4am and be in the field by five, hoeing cotton and soybean until eleven o'clock, for two dollars an hour. The summer's heat was so dangerous we'd be home by noon. Ruth was the foreman watching over us kids hoeing down the quarter mile rows with the local Indians. Completing the half-mile circle, we'd make a beeline for the old beat-up tin water jug, brimming with ice-cold well water. There was a lot of work, but plenty of play as well. Many of our days—and nights—were filled with fishing. At night, we'd sit on five-gallon buckets under the yard light, surrounded by insects of all types, skinning catfish we'd just pulled in from the trot line.

Often we'd leap up, waving our arms about our heads, knife still in hand, as the insect-eating bats swooped too close, chasing the juicier, heavy, bugs closer to the ground. It was a young boy's heaven, and my fondest and best childhood memories were created there in Uncle Ray and Aunt Ruth's simple home. The times we spent together were priceless.

Earlier that year, my parents planned a trip to Disney World in Florida. I was given a choice.

"You can go with us to Disney World or you can go to Oklahoma," My father told me.

"Oklahoma!" I told him without hesitation.

Ray and Ruth still talk about that day when my father and Jo dropped me off. My sneakers were so ragged my toes were sticking out. In fact the tops from the rubber sole to the laces were completely gone. The next day, Ray and Ruth bought me new shoes. I discovered that in the past my uncle and grandfather would talk about how, when my family would visit every year, Carrie and Kathy would be well-dressed and I would look like the "popper's kid." That's the way it was.

Of course I didn't notice the difference in clothes, but in other areas where I knew I was treated differently, it hurt.

As eventually the lights are turned out for the night, so did my good times in Oklahoma come to an end. I returned to my East Texas home with Fred and Jo, and life continued as usual. My best friend Vance lived hours from me. So I latched onto any teenager of the Kingdom Hall who would have me. Getting out of the house was a priority.

In the summer of '79, I was fifteen and Mark and I were running the roads of Beaumont, Texas. Mark, with his curly blond hair, exuded charisma and confidence, but was also known to be a compulsive liar. It was okay though; he was a Witness. He lived in Woodville, just 12 miles up the road, and drove a beautiful, baby blue Lincoln Continental; his father worked at the Ford dealership. We had met up with several Witness friends earlier that day and were headed back at dusk.

I hadn't spent much time with Mark, but I took breaks away from the house whenever I could. It was in part this drive that created the volatile evening I was about to encounter. Our Witness friends gave us a six-pack of beer while we were in Beaumont. Though we were both under age, I suppose they felt we deserved a break.

I probably drank no more than two beers, but was well lit. The alcohol lowered my inhibitions, and that's exactly what I needed. I could never *get into it* with my father or Jo. I seldom gave my opinion or said what was on my mind. I was afraid of confrontation. Just good Witness training, I suppose. When I was asked if I wanted one thing over another my most common response was "I don't care."

I don't care was a safe answer. I learned early that what I cared about never mattered if the decision involved other family members anyway.

Mark dropped me off at the house and sped down the dirt road, his baby blue disappearing into the dark. I waltzed in, got comfortable, and called Dad to come to the living room to ask him a question.

I had been corresponding for a while with a girl I'd met at a Jehovah's Witness Assembly in Oklahoma City, and wanted to call her.

"No," my father said.

With a head of beer courage built up, I wasn't ready to just give in and walk away. Besides, I didn't really want to talk to this girl. There was someone else I wanted to speak to and that desire had been building up inside me for several years.

"I want to try and call my mom," I told him.

He looked at me like he just realized I was drunk. But that wasn't it; he was floored. I had gone years without even a peep about my partying, demonized, long-lost mother, and I just threw him a curve ball. I had just enough beer to give me the strength or nerve to stand up to him and say, more or less, *I've known you and Jo for a while now and I can't take it anymore. Now I want to find my mother.* My dad seemed insulted. He had worked so hard to keep me from her; to him it was as if I was ungrateful for all he went through to save my life. All he gave for me: the blood, the sweat, the tears, the ulcers, and the drained bank accounts: all to help him bring back his son. He became incensed and began berating me.

"You got it good here in this house and you better start appreciating it…"

Though my valor was wearing down fast, I did manage to get out that I was tired of the way Jo had treated me most of my life.

"Let me tell you something," He said pointing his finger. "I remember Jo saving her change just so she could buy you a coat with a hood on it!"

I remember thinking: *of course, she spent all your cash on her own daughters' clothes.* By this time though, I dared not speak. He had quickly corralled me, and softened any backbone I possessed. As usual, I sat there, and I took it. The beer just wasn't enough.

"I've seen your own momma say, 'I wish I'd never had this kid' and then throw you ten feet across the room onto the bed," he told me.

"Well, if she didn't want me why did she keep taking me?"

"Because she was trying to get at me. She wanted you so she could hurt me," he proclaimed. "Your mother is a conniver. I know her. I've seen her stand there, bold face lyin', and be cryin' the whole time."

I could feel my entire spirit draining from my body. Not only was I being put in my place, but I had never heard these new evils. He stood there and forcefully explained just what an ingrate I was, his finger stabbing the air throughout the rant.

"How old are you?" he asked.

"Fifteen—"

"Well, as old as you are, don't you think if your momma wanted anything to do with you, she would've already found you?"

I just sat there, staring at the floor. In my heart of hearts I knew he was right. He could shout all the propaganda he wanted, but I couldn't deny the fact that I was within a year of getting my driver's license and my mother had not even tried to contact me since I was a small child. Inside I was humiliated, devastated: put in my place once again.

He dealt another blow: "even the woman she called 'Mom' told me you'd be better off with me!"

After his many sharp words, he could smell that I was weak, staggering, cowering there on the sofa; he finally drew his dagger and went in for the kill.

"And I know one time, your momma went horseback ridin' with some guy and got bucked off. And this guy raped her."

My mind stalled. *That's not what I just heard, is it? I need to— My mother was raped…?*

My mind shifted to reverse on the freeway. Brain cells were falling over each other. I couldn't make my tongue work.

I'd never heard this before, and I knew I didn't want to hear the rest.

I was already beaten and wanted to escape. *A story about my mother being raped? Do I have to sit here?*

"The thing is: she *bragged* to me that she didn't really get knocked out. She only pretended to be, because she wanted him to do it."

I couldn't move.

"Now that's the kind of people your momma used to hang around with," he said, making his last stab.

I was sick. I was lost. I just wanted to get out of that room.

"If I hadn't taken you, there's no tellin' what would have happened to you!"

He must have felt as though he'd just hit a home run and knocked some sense into me, because he stopped there. Quiet filled the room as I could hear Jo in kitchen carefully and quietly stacking dishes as she listened. I didn't know what do or say. What could I say: *you're right; my mother certainly was a slut?*

Still staring at the floor, I lifted myself from the couch and dragged my battered body upstairs. My legs were iron weights as I took each giant step to the second floor and finally to my bedroom. I didn't know what to think.

How could my mother be so sick? I thought.

I sat on the bed staring at the wall. Eventually, I lay down and cried myself to sleep. All I knew was that I didn't know. I was confused, lost, trapped. This was my life and there was no-one to rescue me.

Once again, my mother was pushed from my mind. At this point it didn't matter if she was evil or not. When my father first told me she was demonized, I knew he had moved us from place to place in order to keep her from finding me. I was very young then. At this time, though, I was a teenager, and he made a very good point in my adolescent mind.

By this time, she had had plenty of time and resources to find me. That is, if she really wanted to. I was sure that no-one I was living with cared about me and now it seemed obvious my mother had decided I wasn't worth the trouble either. I felt discarded and abandoned, and it wouldn't be long before he and Jo would make sure I had an understanding of just what my place was.

Less than two years later, my father accused me of burdening the family once again. I was almost seventeen, working as a carpenter's helper during the summer break. Having worked on their house for so long, I learned many skills. My services were sought after by anyone who witnessed my work ethic. If my father taught me anything, it was to work hard. And when it came to physical labor, I was your man.

He was outside in the dirt drive, fiddling with his truck. I asked him if I could do something or go somewhere. His reply is implanted in my memory, simply because of his bizarre reaction and because of the events which followed. There was no answer to my question.

"We're havin' to bend over backwards just to get along with you," he snapped at me with his heavy jowls.

I was dumbfounded. At the time I had no idea he was even upset with me, much less having to *bend* so much because of me. He had nothing else to say. That was it. No explanation, no example of what I had done wrong. I felt like I had just been sucker punched and kicked in the stomach. I immediately withdrew.

That night I kept to myself. I only went down for food. I stayed in my room and I searched and searched. I thought through the few days prior and just couldn't figure out what

I'd done. I had no clue what was eating him, and I wasn't about to ask.

I thought about it, weighed my options, and came to one conclusion. If it's that tough to have me around, then that's one thing I can fix. The next day I went down for breakfast and didn't see him anywhere; I was relieved. But it wasn't long before Jo came into the kitchen.

"Well, I guess I'm leaving," I told her.

That was it. I figured I had been in their cold home long enough, why should I bother staying. Carrie made it out at seventeen, so could I.

It was obvious: if I was not welcome and they had to "bend over backwards" just to get along with me, why not stop everyone's suffering?

"Why?" Jo asked.

I then explained to her what he told me the day before.

She laughed under her breath and then smiled. "Well, your daddy's been going through some difficult stuff lately."

It was odd how it was almost funny to her. She didn't seem surprised or concerned. It was as if she knew exactly what was going on and it was no big deal. To this day I have no idea what I'd done to give him the backache. I may never know the catalyst. I will say that Jo continued to try and ease my feelings, but by the time she was done, I knew I had to get out of there.

"It's a shame you're leaving. I thought we were just starting to build a relationship," she told me.

I thought: *where the hell am I? I'm seventeen years old and you think we're just now starting to have a relationship?*

I had lived in the same house with this woman for *fourteen years*. Did she not realize how much I needed a relationship with her the whole decade prior?

In the space of twenty-four hours, my father told me I'm too difficult to live with and my stepmother confirmed what I'd felt for years: that she didn't care about me. I knew it; I felt it. For years I was treated as an outsider, and now my only choice was to run as far and fast as I could. How can you not have a relationship with a child in your own home and still *care* about him?

Needless to say, I left. I passed the eleventh grade and I quit school; my father had no problem with it, Armageddon was coming soon anyway. I moved in with my friend, Dale, and his family in Beaumont. Dale helped me get a job as a mason tender where he worked. The owners and many of the employees were Witnesses, so I was right at home.

Though the freedom to make my own decisions and create my own life was the fresh air my soul needed, it wouldn't be long before I returned to the indoctrinated abyss. And once again, I put my father's nerves on edge, just as my mother once did.

Chapter 4

Any day is a good day to die

Living in Beaumont was definitely a nice break from the Witness rigors of my father's home. Preaching door-to-door only a handful of times, my weekends were filled with movies and scuba diving with Dale; Monday nights were set aside for roller-skating. It was a welcome break from the status quo I had lived for years. The problem was the girl.

After about a year, at eighteen years old, I began dating a young girl, whose family we had known from the time my father stealthily moved us to Fayetteville, Arkansas. I remember walking the cold, shallow stream with her and her sister and my stepsisters near their home. Between the walls of the tall, green trees, the sharp water patiently sought the oceans. Being only six at the time, I feel certain they were trying to lose me in their trek as I was constantly playing catch-up. My stepsister Carrie and her older sister (also named Carrie) were very good friends. Still, in my mind's eye, I see her entire family at their trailer house on the hill in the Ozarks.

It was her stepfather who suggested we look at moving to the Woodville area from Houston. As I lived in Beaumont, she still lived in the Woodville area. Once we began dating seriously, I moved back into my father's home to be closer to her. Though my drive to work was at least an hour each way, it was worth it to be closer to the girl of my heart.

Before long, I asked her to marry me. Three months is all it took for us to feel certain we wanted to spend the rest of our lives together. It was the feeling of love I had searched for all my life. At eighteen years old, I felt certain marriage would fill the void. With youth comes the folly of the heart; we were wed in November 1982.

It was a very joyous time for me. I thought I would finally have the warmth of the truly loving relationship I had missed for so long. Though the ominous signs started early, I was blind to them.

"I think you're gonna have headship problems." My father calmly told me one night. It was one of the few times he sat down with me for a father-son chat.

He reminded me of the importance of a submissive wife. In the Jehovah's Witnesses it's the man who makes the decisions and runs the family—who has the "headship."

Taking the submission point of view out of the situation, my father was still correct. She was the first girl I asked and the first to say yes. I knew he was right about her attitude, but my desire rationalized my concerns; I held my course.

Dale approached me at work one day and begged me not to marry. "I already bought two acres and a trailer-house," I told him.

"I'll move in with you."

"You're gonna drive an hour to work every day?" I said sarcastically.

Dale was a bit on the lazy side. His clothes would be strewn across his bedroom floor and each morning he'd pick up one shirt after the other and sniff it to discover what was wearable. I knew there was no way he was going to spend years getting up at five in the morning. And honestly, there wasn't anything he could have said to change my mind.

What I told him next sums up my entire life to that point.

"I just want someone to come home to," I told him.

I had spent most of my life craving that which was absent: love. I had been lonely and rejected for so many years, and I finally felt I had found *it*: someone to love me. Little did I know that marriage does not guarantee a loving relationship.

It had been four years since the night my father and I locked horns over my mother. The span of a kid growing from fourteen to eighteen is a lifetime. I had forgotten about the night I pulled myself upstairs to cry myself to sleep, and I wanted to share my joy.

"I'd like to invite my mother to the wedding," I told my father.

I didn't realize it at the time, but today I'm sure his blood boiled. There I was: an eighteen-year-old *adult* (if that's what you call it). I wanted the right to invite my own mother to my wedding; to what I thought would be the happiest day of my life. It may be lucky for me, I told him, while my bride-to-be was there in the room.

"Okay. I'll try and make some phone calls," he answered, with a smile.

He immediately sprang into action. It seemed odd that, after so many years of saying he had no idea how to find her, he was able to act so quickly and confidently. So erased was she from our lives that he had thrown away all records of anything relating to her. At least that's what he had told me for years.

He marched up to his bedroom and returned thirty or forty minutes later with *new information*. It was like magic. He told me he was able to find old friends of my mother's family who owned some cabins or a trailer park of sorts.

"They said your mom overdosed on drugs, was committed

to a mental institution, and died," he explained in a mournful voice.

I let out a long sigh. For years he'd told me my mother was a demonic abuser, and now he was telling me she's dead.

Needless to say, hearing of my mother's demise was upsetting. I quickly recovered, however, because I knew for certain that I was about to marry a Christian girl, a Jehovah's Witness, and we were in love and would live a blissful life. Besides, even if the relationship was a rocky one, we knew Armageddon was due within about twenty years; then we would both be in Paradise and heading to perfection. I knew it would all work out.

With my lifelong training, I felt sure my mother was most likely demonized anyway, even if she was still alive. So the wedding plans continued and the festivities went without a blip. After all, my mother was dead. I knew; my father told me so. It seemed she had died in the same state my father had left her—partying to the end.

The first three months of my new marriage were great, but our happiness soon went south.

"All men are creeps, all men are the same, and you're no exception," she began telling me on a regular basis. We constantly fought about sex. Sex and money—there was never enough for one or the other of us.

"The Bible says to give your mate his due!" I'd complain.

"It also says everything in moderation!" She'd shout back.

It was obvious we had each brought our own unsettling baggage into an immature union.

A year went by as we fussed and cried, then made up time and again. My mother had faded to the back of my mind as life took hold of all my time and energies.

Our daily concerns became more focused on how we

could get our grocery budget low enough to be able to pay the electric bill. I remained a devout Witness, attending five meetings each week and knocking on doors every weekend, proclaiming my truth to the masses.

We were very proud of our little trailer house on two acres. Two bedrooms, one bathroom, complete with faux furniture, for about fourteen thousand dollars. What else could two country kids ask for?

My mother-in-law came to visit one weekend, which was always welcome. I was more comfortable around her than my stepmother, and had no problem approaching her with my relationship questions concerning her daughter. They were visiting in the living room as I was on a mission searching the whole house for who-knows-what. Focused and determined, I probably became the comic relief of the afternoon. Entering the last untouched room, I dropped to the floor and searched under our bed. Opening each drawer of the dresser, I ran my hands through all the clothes. Then I set eyes on the sliding closet doors.

Pulling one door open, I explored the floor, and shelf, then parted the hanging clothes. I moved to the other door and, irritated, I slammed it to the opposite side. As the door banged against the jamb, a flash of white passed through my vision, just to my right. My hand jetted out to catch the falling object, and missed. Kicking my leg out wildly, I tried to break its fall. It all happened so fast, and yet seemed to happen in slow motion. Before it was over I knew the outcome. A hundred pieces of Milky, white glass scattered across the room.

"SHIT!" I yelled, in pain.

"Are you okay?" My wife's voice echoed through the trailer.

Since I was not in the habit of cursing, they both came to

the room thinking I may have injured myself.

I couldn't respond, nor could I move. I stood there staring at the floor. My mother's beautiful white vase, given to me by my aunt, had fallen onto the rail of the sliding door. It was as if the memories already denied me were nothing more than tiny white shards, scattered across the carpet. Little sharp, painful, reminders of a past I didn't even know. I was nineteen, and I felt as though I had just lost my mother again.

My wife asked, "Are you okay?"

"Yeah—" I lamented.

I cleaned up my mother's remains and threw them in the trash, much as my father had done with her memory years earlier. My heart broke that night. I mourned the loss of my mother; I cried.

In 1985 joy did enter my heart in the form of a beautiful daughter. With life's new demands and struggles, thoughts of my mother once again took a back seat. With a wonderful new life in our home, I had hoped parenthood would bring my wife and me closer together. Instead, it added tensions of a new type.

Two years later, the Texas oil boom fell flat, and with it the economy and jobs. Bills went unpaid and I was forced to look elsewhere for income.

We moved to New Jersey, where the construction boom was well under way. After another year of dysfunctional marriage, we finally separated in 1988.

My wife and daughter moved back to East Texas, over a thousand miles away. The love I so desperately needed and desired was missing, after all.

Though I was relieved to be out of the relationship, I grieved for my daughter. It was in this little blonde girl that I found true, unconditional love. Her absence left a huge emp-

tiness in my life and brought on a tremendous depression.
Speaking to her on the phone would leave me in bed for two
or three days, irritating my employer. I sent her cards to send
back to me to prevent the communication between us from
stagnating. But at three years old, it's just not the same. It was
probably as difficult for her as for me.

Alcohol became my sedative of choice, numbing me
enough to smile and disregard reality. Though I didn't delve
into serious drugs, my sexual partners were as numerous as
the bottles I finished off. It was a welcome change to engage
women who *wanted* to explore the erotic side of my being.
Even as pleasure satisfied my body and soothed my foggy
head, that little Devil in the back of my mind continued to
remind me of my Watchtower training. I knew the consequences, but I was tired of the pain of life; I had given up.

I knew the path I had chosen led me away from God as I
had been taught since my birth. It seemed obvious that I was
not supposed to be happy or live a normal life free from loss
and sorrow. I knew without doubt that I was a dead man walking. I was dead to my family, dead to my friends, and dead to
God. The only consolation I had was that I wouldn't suffer
much longer, for the generation of 1914 was dying off. I knew
that Armageddon would be upon us before that generation
was gone. The end was near and my suffering would be over.
Then I could rest.

This out-of-control lifestyle, of course, led to my being
disfellowshipped from the Jehovah's Witnesses and finally to
my divorce. It was as if my life had taken the same tragic
course as my mother's. I feared, as a child, inheriting her
demonic ways, and as an adult my childhood fears seemed a
certainty.

Over the next few years the depression was great. My

marriage had failed, and I lost my beautiful daughter. My father and stepmother would no longer speak to me and all my friends were required to shun me as long as I was not in good graces with the Watchtower. Raised as a Witness with their shunning policies, I was left alone, just as I had been in childhood.

I was an emotional wreck and I went through life, there in New Jersey, hitting one wall after another, falling down again and again. More than once, I grew tired of waiting for God to take me.

One day, uncharacteristically sober, I lay on the floor of my one-bedroom house. The sun's warmth, through the window, struck my body unnoticed. The tears flooding my eyes distorted the focus on any object, refracting the ceiling light into twinkling stars. An emotional overload was taking its toll as I begged God to explain. I couldn't understand why, after doing the best I could to live up to his standards, my life was so unbearable. Why could I find no happiness? I rolled on the floor and cried much as I did as a child begging for my mother. The pain of loss was more than I wanted to continue to experience. I took my pistol, pressed it to my own temple, felt the cold, round barrel resting there, waiting.

I dared God to take my life before I took it myself, and pulled the trigger half way. That day, Bryan Lee McGlothin died and all evidence of him vanished as he was reborn. Putting the gun down, I lay for forty-five minutes, curled into a fetal position, until I was emotionally and physically drained. I wondered if I looked silly from God's point of view. I decided any day was a good day to die; *I'll just wait on Him.*

Chapter 5

It wasn't easy for you as a kid

As I grew into adulthood, I didn't want to think of myself as "poor me." As difficult as my life may have been, I considered it just that: life. My father raised me to "be a man" in the traditional sense. A *man* must be strong. A *man* takes it. A *man* doesn't show emotion. He didn't believe you were working unless you were sweating. He seemed satisfied when I quit school to become a mason tender and later a bricklayer.

Events in our lives shape us. Nietzsche said, "That which does not destroy me makes me stronger;" I believe that to be the absolute truth. Some people become hardened, others weak.

Lance Armstrong, I feel, is the perfect example. The pain he experienced battling his cancer was much greater than the pain he endures biking though treacherous mountains in France. He was hardened by his experience and is stronger today because of it.

Emotional pain is no different. Either you let it beat you down, or you allow it to build you into a stronger individual, and perhaps a less sensitive person. After being beaten down for so long, I decided to be strong, and so I put the hardships and emotional turmoil behind me and began to look forward. I felt that focusing on a sense of injustice made me weak. As a result, I was forced to reexamine my life, take control, and turn away from victimhood.

Two vital events in my life made me realize who I really was and what my life was truly about.

In February 1990, my grandfather, Buck, died. My father, Jo, Kathy and Carrie drove to McLoud from Texas for the funeral. I was still living in New Jersey and flew in for the service. Though I was not afforded the relationship with my grandfather that my cousins enjoyed, I still felt very close to my father's father.

My dad and I, along with two of my cousins, Carl Dean and Michael, drove to the cemetery the day before Buck's burial. The digger had called and said he was having problems locating the other graves. My grandmother and Uncle Everett, who were hit by a drunk driver, were already buried there, and he couldn't locate the exact spot for the new grave.

Gliding over the muddy road in my father's Bonneville, everyone stared through his own window. As we arrived at the country cemetery, we saw the gravedigger in his mucky overalls, standing next to his backhoe with his hands on his hips and a confused look on his face.

Exiting the car, we reluctantly pulled ourselves towards the malformed hole in the earth next to my grandmother's and uncle's headstones. Before we reached him the digger called out to us.

"Ground's so wet, my hole keeps cavin,'" He said.

We stopped in our tracks, overwhelmed by horrid disbelief. What caught my eye first was the mud-smeared red cloth. Next to it, caked with mud, almost too small to be real, was a human skull.

My grandmother was buried in her favorite red dress, and the man had dug over too close and partially exhumed her. My father was enraged, horrified. He stumbled back and turned, fighting his tears, not wanting us to see his emotion.

"I'm awful sorry about that," the digger said.

My father couldn't speak as he staggered back to the car with me and my cousins in tow.

"I'll get it taken care of!" The man shouted.

A few words were said about the ignorance of the digger as we drove way.

Riding in the front with my father, I could see a tear following the outline of his cheek. I had never seen my father show any emotion, and I felt helpless. I needed to do something to help him—anything, I thought—if nothing else just to let him know that I was there. He was driving with his left hand, his right on the seat of the car, I reached over to hold his hand to try and comfort him the only way I knew.

As soon as my fingers touched the palm of his hand, he jerked his hand away. He never looked away from the road, and never said a word. There was silence all the way back to the house. My father reminded me without a word: *men* don't do that. I suppose his pain made him strong.

Buck was laid in the ground, finally, next to his wife and son, to rest beside them. I saw many relatives there that I had not seen in years. It didn't make any difference though. Most of them were Witnesses; I had been disfellowshipped and was therefore shunned.

Back at my Uncle Ray's house, my father asked to speak with me alone. I followed him around Buck's yellow one-bedroom house, and my father spoke to me in a way he had never spoken to me before. I was almost twenty-six years old and we were only now having our second, serious, father-son talk.

Buck had left my father that little yellow house along with an acre of land. He gave his inheritance to my cousin Michael.

"I didn't think you'd ever want to live out here anyway," he explained.

He was probably correct in his assumption. I had lived in Houston and just across the Hudson from New York City, so I couldn't see myself living in McLoud, even though I had considered returning to the place of my happiest memories.

"Ray said he'd give you an acre anytime, if you wanted it," he told me.

"That's fine," I replied. And I thought, *well, that's nice. He wanted to let me know what he had done with his inheritance.* This was really fine, Michael was a great guy, and had done much more for our grandfather than I had. But Dad didn't stop there.

"I want you to know, that I realize it wasn't easy for you as a kid."

I stood there, silent.

"Jo was pretty rough on you, I know. At times I even thought of getting out myself," he confessed.

His words were foreign; I looked hard at him to make sure they were coming from his mouth. All those times I wished, prayed, that my father would stand up for me; I needed his support so many times, but he was never there. He'd known exactly what I was going through, but did nothing.

"I was just lonely," he said. "I guess we all make decisions in our lives that don't work out the way we'd like them to."

"That's okay," I said, concealing my turmoil. *The one time I might have heard some real answers from him, I say it's okay! No. It's not okay...*

I wrote it all off, and now he was telling me it wasn't my imagination. I had turned my back on what I thought were weak spots in my character. I convinced myself I was just being oversensitive, a sissy boy. Now I was forced to re-examine my youth: something I was not ready to deal with.

I had already been through several years of depression after my divorce. Losing my daughter tore me apart emotionally. I was still disfellowshipped from the Witnesses to boot. Most of my family members at the funeral wouldn't even speak to me. Now I was forced to take another look at my life. This didn't help, though it did reaffirm my suspicions of being emotionally and mentally abused by him and Jo. I knew, finally, that I was the redheaded stepchild, the black sheep of the family.

The next day I flew home to New Jersey. I had plenty of time to think about the few family members who would speak to me, encouraging me to return to "God's Earthly Organization," the Watchtower. I did miss everyone, and I knew all I had to do was attend their meetings once again, and upon reinstatement, everyone would accept me again. Though they can't see it, it is conditional love.

Returning home was welcome and I began to heal after my grandfather's passing. Alone in my tiny attic apartment, I had plenty of time to ponder my father's words. To think of how he had abandoned me for so many years, right there in his own home. I began wondering if he had forsaken me in other ways. If he was so concerned about protecting me from my abusive mother, why didn't he protect me from my abusive stepmother?

Any trust I may have given my father I buried with my grandfather. My loneliness conjured thoughts of my mother once again and I decided she may be more reachable than he would like her to be. I began searching for her in earnest; after all, she is my mother.

Chapter 6

I resented you

Pyewacket sat on the windowsill every evening as I cooked on the hotplate in my attic apartment in Elizabeth, New Jersey. She was silky black and not much more than a kitten. My girlfriend, Kathy, and I picked her up late October. We hadn't given it a thought, the fact that she was jet black and the perfect sacrifice for Halloween. The woman at the SPCA told us we didn't seem the type to be looking for such an item and cautiously allowed us to adopt. I suppose it was fortunate for us that she hadn't heard my mother was demonized.

The early nineties were difficult for me. Almost a year earlier we had buried my grandfather. I was laid off for about eight months of those two years and only unemployment checks kept me alive. So there I was in my little attic apartment: no car, shunned by family and friends. Occasionally I would receive a letter of support or a phone call from a caring elder or relative, telling me I would never truly be happy until I returned to Jehovah.

It had been almost ten years since my last attempt to locate my mother, and I'm sure my loneliness spurred me, at that time, to find her.

Even though my father told me she died because of her wayward ways, I felt the need to confirm his allegation. Computers were only just taking off and the internet was in its infancy, so I did all my work via snail-mail and phone. I pulled out the notes I had taken over the years by dragging information out of my father: three handwritten pages. Then I called him one more time to try and jolt his memory. He did supply some additional information in response to my renewed interest. Perhaps his new honesty was at least partly genuine. Undoubtedly, though, he knew where this newfound information would lead me: definitely not to my mother.

He was, however, able to open his little bag of tricks and tell me where my grandmother, Lola Mae, was buried; he revealed that she was interred at Forrest Lawn Memorial Park, in Glendale, California.

How this had slipped him for so long I had no clue, though I speculated. I called the memorial park and discovered my grandmother was indeed there and that, in fact, she was buried in a double plot. The second plot was still vacant: a positive sign. Now I knew my mother was not there with her, and this news led me to believe my grandfather might still be alive, too.

I hoped there would be some paperwork concerning the plot, which might have someone's contact information. Speaking with the woman in the cemetery office, I discovered that the second plot was for Bryan, my grandfather, but there was no contact information. Though I had located a new family member, it was not as joyous as I had hoped. I had to start over.

My old notes contained several names my father had given me before, such as G.W. Turner, my mother's uncle, along with Edward Franco, my Aunt Sherry's husband. Then there was the name my father had so vaguely remembered, my mother's husband: Jack Stamper. He had used variations of the name, saying he couldn't really remember how it was pronounced, though he did lean toward "Stamper."

Along with names, he gave me cities: Covina, West Covina, and Glendale, where he thought they had lived. For the first few days, I called information and asked for listings using variations of the names I had recorded.

I called them one by one, feeling like a telemarketer: "Yes, my name is Bryan McGlothin; I'm looking for Mr. Turner who would be related to Angie Mason or McGlothin, or Stamper—" Of course, each time, I would have to give the whole spiel of why I was looking for these people. Everyone was kind enough though, especially one woman who, at the end of our conversation, said she hoped I would find my mother. This effort was to prove fruitless.

Drawing to the end of my notes of names, places and dates, I was all but ready to give up once again. But then I had an idea. Recalling my father's story of my mother's death, I decided I needed a death certificate.

I called California Department of Health Services and requested the forms. After receiving the paperwork I entered my information requesting a death certificate for Angie Lenora Stamper. I sent it along with twenty dollars in late November. Then I waited, regretting what I had done, for close to a month.

Do I really want to know my mother has died? I thought. What a tragic ending that would be, for my mother not to be with Lola Mae, her own mother, in her final resting place— and to be deprived of her son at her own passing. It was a very confusing time for me, but it was not long before I had my answer.

Just after Christmas, I received the envelope from California. I placed it on my little dining table and contemplated what I might find upon opening it. I sat there for a few moments and watched Pye play with a stuffed mouse that was dressed like one of Santa's little helpers. After realizing I had zoned out, I pulled my head from the clouds and slid a knife across the top of the envelope. Upon retrieving the contents I found the receipt and a document. It was dated December 26th 1990, and was titled "Certification of no Record." I took a deep breath and let it out slowly. I knew, at least, that my mother had not died in California. I was happy and relieved, but I knew the search would go on and I had still to face the realities of my dark childhood.

In the meantime, Kathy and I went our separate ways and I was drawn back to the Witnesses. Alone for so long in New Jersey, I began looking for that which I had lost, and like a battered wife returning to her brutish husband, I returned to the mighty Watchtower. I went to meetings three days a week for six months. It was difficult to say the least, since no-one could speak to me, but everyone was welcome to stare. Two of the congregational elders worked with me, helping to keep me on the straight and narrow, while I begged for God's and the Watchtower's forgiveness.

Once reinstated, my family and friends were allowed to associate with me again, and I moved back to East Texas where my father and stepmother lived and, most importantly, where my daughter, then seven, was living.

My dad and Jo were kind enough to allow me to live with them until I found work and figured out what I was going to do with my life. I had worked in Beaumont for several years, and had many Witness friends there as well. But my daughter lived in the Woodville area, and I wasn't sure I wanted to live so far away.

I picked up brickwork in Beaumont with an old employer

and bought two acres once again in Warren. During my marriage to Anna's mother, I made the one-hour drive from Warren to Beaumont for six years, so living in the "Big Thicket" was not out of the question. In any case, I had been living with my father and Jo for three months.

They had their routines down pat. He would go to bed by nine or ten and Jo would read her *Watchtower* or *Awake* magazines as she nibbled peanuts. In the past, she would have been drinking a vodka and coke, but at the time my father was having a problem with his alcohol intake and she didn't want to encourage him. At twenty-eight and still functioning on an East Coast schedule, I couldn't to go to bed that early. There was very little to do there in the country that late at night, so I usually sat in Dad's chair and watched TV while Jo read.

One evening, after my father had retired and I had settled into the usual evening routine, Jo lowered her magazine to her lap, removed her small reading glasses, and started a bit of small talk.

This was fine with me; Jo mellowed out in her older years, so we chatted for a while. Then, just as my father had dropped a bag of sand on my head two years earlier, Jo needed to lift a weight from her own shoulders.

"I want you to know that I realize I was pretty rough on you as a kid… And I'm sorry."

I was speechless all over again. Images of her scolding me as a child rushed through my mind. The emotions returned, ran through the cells of my body. The person who had treated me with such disdain, it seemed, had abandoned her aversion out of the blue. Once again I was dumbfounded, but no less intrigued as to what was to come next.

"The reason I treated you like I did was because I

resented you."

I didn't get it. I was a three-year-old when she married my father. How could she resent a little harmless kid? As my thoughts whirled into a vortex of confusion, she fell silent.

Catch your breath, I thought. *Don't let it end here like you always do—*

"Why did you resent me?" I asked, grasping at the first rational thought I could form.

"Well, when I married your daddy, it was like he threw you in my lap and said, 'Here, you take care of him.'"

At that moment, the lights went on, and I truly understood my childhood. It was as if all the puzzle pieces of a lifetime fell from the sky to the table and spontaneously assembled into a coherent, albeit sad, picture. It all made sense; the actual effect of a father who never made time for me and who made no attempt at a relationship, who belittled me and took no pleasure in my accomplishments. And the other great influence in my early life, the disdainful way Jo treated me in contrast to her own children, did nothing but reinforce my alienation and isolation. At that moment I saw it clearly: the loose ends had finally found one another.

"...and I just didn't appreciate it," Jo continued. "I had two girls of my own. I know I can't do anything to change it, but I want you to know that I'm sorry."

"That's okay," I said, once again.

In my head, I shouted, *why do I keep doing that?*

We might have talked for hours if I had said something more. But I didn't—*couldn't*. I hate confrontation.

On one hand, I thought, Jo was admitting wrongdoing; *Ha! There, you see, you are bad.* But on the other hand, I thought, *good for you, it must have taken a lot of courage to admit that.* But in reality, she placed the fault squarely on her husband.

Still, the conversation was a great landmark on my quest to discover and understand; most of all, it confirmed that I was not merely a weak person. It validated my experience. My father "threw me" to her, as she so eloquently put it. He didn't want anything to do with me.

Years later, two members of his family confided in me and said that abducting me was nothing more than a power play for my father. He felt my mother had ruined his life and he chose to take and withhold what she most wanted and loved.

"Your daddy really didn't want you," I was told.

As hard as it was to hear, I know it's the truth. My father just didn't want me around—except of course, when it came to helping him deliver TVs, clearing land, or building a house. It's obvious now; memory after memory confirms it.

"I swear, sometimes I think you're half mentally retarded," he once shouted at me. I was ten, and I was devastated. I turned and crept behind the backyard fence; I didn't want him to see me cry.

I'm sure he viewed me as a burden, yet no matter how much I encumbered him and his new family, he wasn't about to let his ex-wife have peace of mind—or his own son.

So he denied my mother and me both our happiness, then pawned me off on his new wife. She didn't want me, but felt stuck. Jo's heated anger for being used by her new husband transferred to me, the redheaded stepchild. I wished, for a moment, that I had never heard Jo's words. The truth is always good, but it doesn't mean it's easy.

Seeing my father's true motives did nothing more than fuel the flame of my desire to find my mother. Whether she wanted to hear from her son or not, I was going to find her.

I moved on from the piney woods of Woodville after a serious injury from a fall on a construction site—and another failed marriage to a Jehovah's Witness. I moved to Houston, near my stepsisters, Carrie and Kathy.

During this time, I completed recovery from my accident and was able, at last, to exorcize the Jehovah's Witness Devil that had possessed my conscience since I was born. The deprogramming took years without professional help, but I finally realized I was not a dead man walking. I was alive, and I would become whole.

Once on the road to spiritual, emotional, and mental health, I made many wonderful friends. One companion on my journey was Marilyn, a wonderful British woman who carried the nickname "Miss Manners."

Marilyn taught proper etiquette, all the while emitting an air of royalty. When she dusted her own home it was in a dress and high heels and she was always prepared for a last-minute cocktail party. What I didn't know for some time was that Marilyn and I both carried in our hearts a family mystery.

She had searched for her father for years and finally turned to the Salvation Army for help. She suggested I do the same. I was very surprised; I had no idea the Salvation Army helped people to locate missing family members.

In August 1996, I returned with new passion for seeking my mother, and found at the same time a passion for another woman who entered my life.

Evelyne Tharet, a beautiful and elegant French lady, had caught my eye. I had taken up acting as a hobby at local community theatres and she was spending her free time stage managing at the Actor's Theatre in Houston. We'd bump into each other at the different cast parties and exchanged pleasantries, but I always felt she was several notches above me. After some time, and a couple of drinks, I finally found the confidence to ask her out. Thank God for my fragile courage, she said yes.

From that day, Evelyne and I grew closer as she shared the joys and heartbreaks of my most personal search. Having come from such a large, close-knit family, it was difficult for her to understand the sorrow I had lived through, having sought my mother for decades and experienced the shameful shunning by family and friends. Her gentle and caring soul became a great support during my emotional highs and lows. My search became her search, and most of all, her love became my love.

In our relationship's infancy I called the Salvation Army about the family member search of which Marilyn had spoken. They sent the required forms, which I promptly returned. Evelyne and I went back to life as usual with a bit of electricity in the air, hoping each day for good news.

The letter arrived late the next month. We were hoping to find my mother's address and phone number listed in elegant print. We were not to have that triumph.

All the same, the letter was a positive note: the search would continue. It said they felt they could help locate my mother by approaching the Social Security Office with my dilemma. Following their instructions, I gave a brief version of my story and included copies of different birth certificates and documents. Fingers crossed, I placed another wad of forms in the mailbox, and once again we waited. Having the Salvation Army working with me was a true boost to my enthusiasm.

My excited hopes were, however, tempered by the fear that my mother would not desire a relationship with me. After all, it had been thirty years since she had seen me and, as far as I knew, she never tried to find me. I waited in anticipation and resolved to accept any outcome.

Approximately three months later, we received a response, in which the Salvation Army stated they were regrettably unable to attain the help of the Social Security Office. It seemed par for the course. Once again I had run into an invisible wall barring my way to my mother.

Perhaps, I thought, finding my mother just wasn't in the cards, a taboo possibility outside of the ebb and flow of normal life. I had been physically searching for her for close to fifteen years, and was nearly prepared to lay down my torch and walk away from the quest of my life.

Perhaps this is who I am and always will be, I thought: The Boy Who Never Found His Mother. Perhaps she and I were put here on this earth, in this situation, to learn from separation and desperation. I sat back as life continued its daily forward motion, and until another character, a very important character, crossed my path. I didn't have to wait long.

Chapter 7

Does he know that I'm his mother?

One year after my initial contact with the Salvation Army, in the summer of 1997, Evelyne and I had moved in together and were living behind the Jewish Community Center in Houston. As we matured our relationship into an engagement, we also began a journey of spiritual enlightenment. It was amazingly healing for me to realize I didn't need to preach door-to-door several hours a month to be accepted by God; nor was shunning those who thought differently a necessity for a true Christian. I was experiencing life as I never had; the freedom to nurture a relationship with God without dogma was both enlightening and calming to my entire being. And though my mother was not in my life, I discovered a peace of mind and calm for which I had yearned for years. My life was transformed, thanks to the wonderful, loving soulmate who had blessed my journey. All I needed now was my mother.

My longing for her was expressed in chats with friends and curious strangers alike. All were intrigued by my story of being kidnapped by my father and of searching, even at thirty-three years old, for my mother.

One new acquaintance, a friend of a friend, was particularly intrigued. Though he was twenty years my senior, we became good friends quickly after being introduced that summer by our mutual friend, a vivacious Aussie named Theresa.

She has played the piano in more countries than I can count, and has a knack of carrying any party. At the time, she was moving from one apartment to another, and solicited the help of her friends. That's where and how James and I met and hit it off.

He was a very tall and mellow individual; kindness flowed from his heart just as his silver, shoulder-length hair.

"Did Bryan tell you he's looking for his mother?" Theresa said in her beautiful Aussie accent.

"Are you kidding me?" James replied, and waited to hear more. He shook his head in disbelief as I related my tale. From that day, James and I began building what would become not only a close and caring friendship, but which would change lives.

Over the next month he several times inquired of my story. He seemed genuinely moved by the haplessness of a thirty-something man still searching for his mother.

Theresa and Marilyn always said I seemed an old soul, that I presented myself in a wise and mature way. I considered it life's knocks forcing me to face obstacles and learn to overcome. By this time, I'd seen more than my share of turmoil. Perhaps that's why, even with our age difference, James and I became such wonderful friends.

The River Oaks Grill was packed as we crowded around the grand piano to hear Theresa's magical fingers play the many tunes we loved to sing. It was a regular Saturday night gathering with "T and friends." The wine was great and the company even better. The River Oaks restaurant and bar was our haven from the work week and watering hole of our souls. We shouted to one another over the tunes and song as the night played on. To my right was the beautiful Evelyne, the woman I had grown accustomed to go nowhere without. On my left, my friend James stood holding a fifteen-year scotch on the rocks in one hand and a fine cigar in the other, singing "Summer Time" with more blue than I had ever heard.

After polishing the grand with his velvet voice, he took a sip and a puff and looked directly into my eyes. He said, "You know, I think I can help you find your mother."

His words were the last thing I was expecting that night and I was taken aback as Theresa's smooth ivories faded to the back of my mind. Before replying, I studied his face and wondered: *it's very loud in here. Did I hear him right?*

"What?" I asked.

"I think I can help you find your mother," he shouted as though hearing were my problem.

I always enjoyed relating my chronicle, but never did anyone offer to help find its ending. That really was the whole thing. I had been telling my story for years, without an ending.

"Are you serious?"

"Yes." He said with confidence.

Whether the outcome was good or bad, he felt he could provide me with just that, an ending: *my mother.*

Over the years I'd daydreamed of finding her. Sometimes she was living in Los Angeles and wouldn't answer my letters. Sometimes I would show up at her home, whereupon she'd simply dismiss me, feeling I'd waited to too long to contact her, enjoying a great life without me in which there was no sense in starting a relationship. Other times, in my mind, I'd find her destitute, a broken woman, living out the last of her years in solitude. Upon finding her, she'd cry to the heavens in exuberance, having been reunited with her only child. After years with no conclusion, quite frankly, by this time I didn't expect to come upon any suitable climax. I was resigned to telling and retelling of the mother who was.

"That would be great!" I said.

James smiled, held up his drink as I concurred. "What's her name?"

"Angie."

"Here's to Angie," he proclaimed in toast.

"Yes. Here's to my mother!" I smiled, energized once again for the search.

James was in contact with a private detective of sorts, so private in fact, I never met him (or her). That evening James and I planned on lunch the next day. He had instructed me to bring every bit of information I had on my mother. As Theresa played us into the night, we sang, we danced and toasted to the new search and great friendships.

What an exciting, sleepless night. *What a great friend,* I thought. Evelyne was ecstatic. She carries many precious memories of Christmas mornings and Easter candy, family picnics and motherly love. Though she left Paris more than a decade prior, she rarely missed a weekend phone call with family. My life, on the contrary, raised in a cultish environment with few family or longtime friends, was difficult for her to imagine. The thought of my being reunited with my mother thrilled her. The thought of my life becoming more complete excited her.

That night, the ceiling was my friend as my mind traveled to the unknown future. I was still questioning the outcome; would it be a joyous reunion or another emotional scar to bear?

Less than two weeks after that lunch, James phoned. I suspected nothing as we had shared stories and drinks several times since that inspiring evening. Having run into so many dead ends in my quest, I really didn't expect him to achieve what for me seemed impossible. I had no clue he was about to turn my world upside down.

"Well, my friend, I have some information for you." He said. "Could I come by sometime?"

"Hell yes! I'm here. Come on over." I dropped the phone, overcome by a sensation I had never felt before. *This is it; James has the end of my story. The final chapter.* I couldn't wrap my head around it; it was incredible that this could actually be happening. But then I realized that he declined to offer any information over the phone. *Perhaps my mother is dead. Oh my God, what if she died in a car wreck just last week?*

My anxiety equaled my exuberance as I relayed the call to Evelyne. She was excited, like a young child chasing the ice-cream truck on a hot day, but I knew better. I had been the main character of this long-drawn-out tale for many years, and felt sure it couldn't be this easy. There was no way it was all going to fall together into a nice, happy ending.

My father's words came back to me: *don't you think if your momma wanted anything to do with you, she would've already found you?* I was beginning to think maybe we shouldn't continue. I wasn't sure this was what I wanted. I wasn't sure I was ready for a possible rejection or, for that matter, even to be told she died trying to find me. I was afraid of having to travel to her grave and read on her headstone, *Here rests a broken woman who never had a chance.* At the very bottom it would read: *Have You Seen My Son?*

Evelyne put on some soothing music, Mozart I believe, which I definitely needed. It felt like my nerves were dancing on the shards of my mother's broken vase. James was on his way over as we both waited impatiently for the news.

The doorbell soon chimed and my butterflies went into

hyperdrive. At the door was my towering friend. James only added to my anxiety when he entered in a manner unlike his usual jovial self—like a military notifier in dress uniform, delivering news of a loved one killed in action. Gathering in the living room, we prepared for his news. I leaned on the arm of the sofa as sitting still was impossible. Then, in a serious tone, he uttered the words I had waited a lifetime to hear.

"Well my friend, we found your mother."

I wanted to shout in joy. I wanted to cry. I wanted to slow down. Please, slow down. This was the end. No longer would I be the guy searching in vain for his mother. At that moment, my whole life changed.

"Oh wow." Was all could get out.

Not "wow" as in "let's party," but as in *whoa... I'm not sure I'm ready for this...*

"I'm a little worried, though," he said.

Oh no, here it comes...

"I have her address here, but I couldn't find a phone number." He retrieved from his pants pocket a torn scrap of notebook paper, no more than three inches long. "It's a little odd, but I suppose you can write her," he added, as the paper passed from his fingers to mine.

It was as if he where handing over the map to my Grail quest. He could go only so far and now it was up to me to finish the journey; to obtain the magical elixir to heal the wounds, to break the spell.

Taking the paper from him, I could not take my eyes off the simple little note. It was unfathomable to me that the end of my story was printed on a small, torn piece of paper. All these years, decades of guessing, searching, crying, and there lay my mother in my hand. It seemed only proper that the paper was torn. I hoped she was anxious and not complacent:

daily awaiting my arrival rather than living her life free of the thought of her baby boy, lost so many decades ago.

Embracing James, I thanked him as we waltzed to the door. Evelyne hugged him and kissed his cheeks; how wonderful that the French are always looking for an excuse to kiss! Sensing our emotion, he soon excused himself and we were left there to catch our breath. I was in a trance. I had searched for so long, and within two weeks he delivers my mother to me. I had in my possession, in my hand, all I needed to tell her how I really felt. I was thirty-three years old and I was not sure I had ever told her, "I love you."

That evening I began drafting my letter. I discarded page after page, littering the floor with crumpled yellow drafts of tearful words. What do you tell your mother when you haven't seen her in over thirty years? The finest words I could conjure with my eleventh grade education could not convey the many emotions running through my body. The letter would not be typed, I decided, but printed in my own hand. When she opened my letter I wanted her to be as close to me as possible.

Once my letter was sent, I still couldn't suppress my excitement and anticipation about her reaction when she discovered that I had found her. I began calling my friends and stepsisters, and proclaimed my world-shaking news. What I didn't understand was that mine was not the only world about to be shaken.

Hearing the news, my father sounded surprised—and subdued. At this time I didn't understand the disdain he still carried for her, nor the secrets he carried for himself. Not only was he unimpressed with my victory, he began building the wall to end our distant relationship.

I asked him for more information about the first two years

of my life. I wanted to know everything. I wanted to get it all down on paper. Even though he had told me several things in the past, the subject did not allow us to sit down and have an hour-long conversation about where I was, when, and why. I always felt self-conscious talking about *her* with him. Though it would stand to reason that I had every right to do so—she is my mother—my early training to regard her as unspeakably evil formed an awkwardness and a deep fear of conversation about this sinister subject.

Now, however, finding my mother gave me new resolve and strength. I was an adult and decided I needed to know even if it was uncomfortable for my father. This was all about me. My life was about to become complete and I needed him to fill in a few gaps. I visited him once to get the chronology of events down pat.

He worked his mental archives to come up with different dates and sorted information, but he wasn't very successful. I understood, it was thirty years ago, after all. I still pushed, hoping to jog his memory, but he seemed to be saying the same old things told to me in years past.

"Your mother took off with you in August of '64," he said.

That was one date he never forgot, understandably.

"I dyed my hair and grew a mustache one time," he added.

I thought, *this is new,* as he told me how he followed my mother to her mobile home in Southern California.

"She was with some guy," he continued. "That time, I went back to Oklahoma without you."

Now we're getting somewhere, I thought. I hadn't heard that one before.

His building irritation became obvious in his face and his terse replies. I soon gave up. Returning to my daily activities, my concentration on the tasks at hand was limited. All I could think of was my mother and how I fit into her life thirty years ago—and the looming fear of receiving no reply at all, or a response of disdain for not having found her earlier. For days I was a jumble of excited emotions and edgy nerves as I awaited my destiny.

Growing more and more impatient I called my father again, hoping he had regained lost memories since our last conversation. I needed answers and he had them. This time, though, he would provide more than answers. He presented me with more questions and an uneasy knot in my stomach.

"I thought I told you all this last time," he growled.

It was obvious he was growing weary of my interviews. Normally, I would have dropped it as a lost cause. But I was in possession of an inquisitive drive that wouldn't relax its grip on my psyche.

"Well, I'm sorry. I'm not very organized and I keep coming up with more questions to ask."

I was being truthful. Even today Evelyne cringes at the thought of organizing me. She tries, yes she does. But it's like cleaning house. In a few days you have to do it all over again.

So I dug in and refused to let him go easily. I could tell he was becoming more irritated as he again mentioned my mother arriving at his father's house with a guy on a motorcycle. She was there looking for me, and as Buck opened the door, *BAM!* The guy introduced his fist to my grandfather's face.

I have a couple of cousins who agree that this sounds a bit skewed. Our grandfather was a big man and definitely not afraid to tie it up with anyone. Buck would have torn the guy up; one of them surely would have ended up in the hospital. The story just wasn't right.

Buck told me once about his brother Lige; he loved to fight. One night they were riding the buckboard home after a bar brawl. I don't know if my grandfather was in the fight, but Lige had to pick the other guy's flesh from his teeth. Lige was later shot and killed in a bar. The McGlothins were pretty tough characters back in their day.

My father continued to rant about the sins of my mother and told another story I'd heard before.

"You mother went horseback riding one time," he started.

I was seeking answers to new questions, and started to cut him short. I didn't want to hear the story of my mother being raped again anyway. But then his next sentence opened my eyes and made me realize how much I didn't know. And it was all in his head. I didn't say a word as he continued his story.

"It was with two of my cousins."

What, I thought. *I've heard this story before! It's always been some guy—*

"She was either raped or had sex with 'em. I don't know, but that's the kind of stuff your momma did!"

I was silent. I suddenly became that little boy who was afraid to bring up those dangerous topics.

"Who was it?" I carefully asked.

"It was Sammy and Junior. Gloria's boys."

Oh, my God. He's told this to me before. But, now—now it's not "some guy;" it's two men—his own cousins! And what is this, "She was raped or had sex with them?"

He had told me before that she *let* the guy *rape* her and then *bragged* to him about it. There was no "I'm not sure." There were no "two guys." It was one. One guy and she let it happen. And now it was two of his own cousins, and he's suddenly not sure what happened.

How does a man not know if his own wife has been raped?

I let him off the phone easily after that. I was flabbergasted. I didn't understand how his story could be so different. To this day I want to ask him, "What did you do?"

I keep thinking, *If one of my family members even had sex with my wife, much less rape her, there's going to be a fight!*

I don't condone violence, but what would you do? My father never told me what he did. I've since talked to his family about it, and they remember an incident. Two of them recall it involving Sammy, but no-one remembers my father doing anything about it. One thing is for certain, because of this rape or adultery—whatever it was—my mother was disfellowshipped from the Jehovah's Witness Organization. From that point she was shunned by all Witnesses, including those of her own family, just as I was. And this allowed my father to get rid of her for good.

One Watchtower publication, *Our Kingdom Ministry 2002*, states as follows, under the heading "Relatives Not in the Household:"

> *The situation is different if the disfellowshipped or disassociated one is a relative living outside the immediate family circle and home... It might be possible to have almost no contact at all with the relative. Even if there were some family matters requiring contact, this certainly would be kept to a minimum, in harmony with the divine injunction to "quit mixing in company with anyone" who is guilty of sinning unrepentantly (1 Cor. 5:11).*

> *Loyal Christians should strive to avoid needless association with such a relative, even keeping business dealings to an absolute minimum.*

Notice even ones "disassociated," or baptized ones who simply decided the teachings of the Witnesses were not for them, were shunned as unrepentant sinners. My mother, being disfellowshipped, had no-one to turn to.

In the Jehovah's Witnesses Organization, there are only two ways to dissolve a marriage. The first one is death; no news there. The second is adultery. If your mate engages in sex with someone besides yourself, you can get a *scriptural divorce*, as the Witnesses call it. Without the scriptural divorce you can get the regular old run-of-the-mill divorce at the courthouse, but you had better not remarry. If you remarry without that scriptural divorce from the Watchtower, you will then be an adulterer. You will most likely be disfellowshipped, and cast out from the others.

So now I have to ask, on what grounds was my mother disfellowshipped? If my father doesn't know if she was raped or had sex, how could the elders who disfellowshipped her know? Surely, she wouldn't have been disfellowshipped if she was raped? Why, after all these years, just as I am about to find her, did my father change his story? I decided I'd wait, let him cool down, and bring the topic up at a later date.

It was one of the few times Evelyne and I were invited to my father and Jo's home in Dickinson, Texas. I was a little uneasy as I had told him a few months earlier that we were moving in together.

"That's not the way I raised you," he told me.

I understood and respected his viewpoint, but I was living my life—not his. A short time after we began living together, we filed for common law marriage, which seemed to ease his conscience.

All three of us kids were to visit along with some of the grandkids. I think I had only been in their home once before, and it was evident where my father and Jo stood concerning me. As most parents get older, they fill their home with photos of their handsome family: memories and glimpses of the kids and grandkids they don't get to see nearly enough. There must have been at least twenty-five pictures throughout Dad and Jo's living room, but of all those pictures, only one picture was of my daughter, Anna, with me, and one other was of Anna alone. Otherwise, the place looked like a shrine to my stepsisters and their children: photos at different ages and different places, as adults vacationing with our parents, a time-capsule of "the girls." Though it made Evelyne uncomfortable, I was used to it; that was just the way it was.

The evening was going well and, after dinner, my father pulled me to one side and said he had something for me. He put a large, open envelope full of papers and old photos into my hand. Several photos were of him and me, taken in the mid-sixties—back when they added color to black and white prints. Perhaps he hoped the contents would answer some of my questions and save him from another interview. I thanked him and we soon left for home.

Once home, I scoured through the contents and found some amazing things. Along with the pictures of me and my father there were photos of people of whom he'd said he had no knowledge. The envelope also contained two notebooks in my mother's writing.

They were both written during Jehovah's Witness conventions: speaker notes. One contained a letter from my mother to her parents, dated September 11th 1963, that was never mailed. She and my father had driven to California to attend the "Everlasting Good News" Jehovah's Witness convention at the Rose Bowl. On the road back to Oklahoma, my mother wrote a short letter.

As far as I know I'm pregnant. But not for sure yet.
Since I left Oklahoma, I gained 8 pounds. I weigh 113
lbs.

Even though she was tall and slender, she was only sixteen years old.

It was so amazing for me to see her thoughts on paper. The other notebook written at the same time had, in red ink, my name, Bryan Lee McGlothin, and Tracy Mae McGlothin. The latter was to be my name if I were born a girl. On the page opposite the cover containing my name was one of the most beautiful expressions I had seen in my entire existence. Not words, but a kiss. My mother, over her handwritten notes, had placed a kiss of lipstick on the page. It was as if she had sent it to me in a letter, lost in the mail, over thirty years ago. I knew those lips had caressed my cheeks and forehead as a baby. The thought of having lost such tender affection drew tears. My fingers gently stroked her seal of love as I hoped to receive her kisses once again.

The large envelope also contained a short letter from my mother to my grandparents, Buck and Lucille, dated January 24th 1966; I was one and a half years old. It was an example of how my mother communicated with my father during the years he was on the run with me.

In it, she asked them to forward her letter to my father. She writes:

Dear Lucille and all,

I received a letter from Freddie and baby. They are
doing fine, although they have been sick.
Freddie sent me a picture of Bryan and [he] is so

cute. And he sure has grown.

I've written Freddie another letter. Would you mail it as soon as you can?

Take care and tell everyone hello for me.

As Ever,

Angie

It was obvious my mother was being very cordial in hopes of getting the letter to my father in a timely fashion.

The envelope contained other documents and letters, including her birth certificate, but the most moving was dated June 23rd 1972; I had just turned eight years old.

Of all the possessions I had relating to or coming from my mother, this one ripped my heart out. I still don't understand why my father gave it to me; it's so incriminating. I believe he was divesting himself of information he knew I would soon discover.

The letter speaks of my relationship with the Jehovah's Witnesses. She speaks of me "in service," which is what the Witnesses call knocking at your door. "Theocratic Ministry School" is another reference she makes, where Bible students give talks from the platform to improve their speaking skills for when they knock on your door. My mother writes:

Fred,

I received your most welcome letter. Thank you very much for the papers that Bryan did. They are really good. He prints really nice. Also thank you for the pictures. He is the cutest little guy I have ever seen. I love him so very much. I hope someday you'll find it in your heart to let me see him. Does he know that I'm his mother? Have you told him about me?"

After reading this, I wondered what type of conscience would allow a man to force his wife to ask such questions: *I hope someday you'll find it in your heart to let me see him.* Even though she was helpless, my father, all the while considering himself a Christian, never found it in his heart to grant her wish.

The last two sentences, I believe, prompted my father to ask me the question that began it all: "You know Jo isn't your momma, don't you?"

In the same letter, my mother continues:

Is he going to be tall? I imagine he's pretty tall now. What grade is he in? Fred, I'm sorry you lost your grandmother. What will happen to your uncle now? My grandmother Mason died March 15th 72 and Mam-maw Turner died the 21st of April, 72.

After what could be considered small talk, my mother again brings up the idea of getting in touch with me.

If you have told Bryan about me, and you don't care, could I send him a picture of me?

I hope that he doesn't have a bad problem with his teeth. Do you think his teeth will be strait? If he needs braces—I could help you get them.

Fred, it was such a long time between letters, could you write more often? Please? Please let me know how Bryan is doing from time to time.

How does he do in the service? Is he shy? Does he

take part in the theocratic ministry school?"
Thank you again,

Angie

My father, beginning when I was only eight, told me repeatedly that he had thrown all my mother's things away. And when I was fifteen, he'd wilted my adolescent spirit by saying, "well as old as you are, don't you think if your momma wanted anything to do with you, she would already have found you?"

Yet she tried and tried, and as late as 1972 she was begging to see me. My father fooled me into thinking she couldn't care less about me. After reading her letter I felt broken. My heart hurt for her; my heart hurt for me. Yet she was not a felon, a drug addict, or a child abuser. If any of these had been the case, my father wouldn't have had any problem going before a judge and getting full custody of me.

The envelope also contained original divorce papers, which had never been signed by my mother. My father obtained the divorce in Louisville, Kentucky; there was no visitation provided for me with my mother.

Patience was not my strong point as I waited to hear back from her. *Please don't let it end here,* I thought. *She's got to want to see me.*

In the meantime, even though I had already irritated my father, I wanted to know why his story changed. In giving me these documents and pictures, surely he didn't think I would just shut up. He must have realized that I would be plagued by questions.

It wasn't easy. I was sure that if I called again there would be fire and brimstone. I felt strengthened by my desire for the truth. I now knew where my mother was and, by God, I wanted information. So I punched in his number and waited for the barbs.

"Hey Dad," I said as cheerfully as possible.

"Yeah," he replied, obviously on guard.

"I'm putting all my notes together and had just a couple more questions if you don't mind."

"What for?"

"Well like I said, I'm trying to fill gaps in my notes—"

"Look!" He barked. "I am tired of talkin' about this. That woman ruined my life, and last time you asked so many questions, I lost two nights sleep! I'm done with it!"

What could I do? What I really wanted to do was blurt out the burning question: *why did you change your story about my mother being raped?*

But I knew there would be no budging him. He was pissed, and he knew I was about to learn the other half of the story; the part he had been hiding for decades. That's why he gave me the folder containing the pictures and documents. He was preparing me in the only way he could for what my mother was about to tell me. Or perhaps she had the letters he wrote her. No doubt he was very uneasy knowing I was about to hear the other side. Maybe he felt when I confronted him with an issue he could say, "Everything I know is in that envelope." Perhaps he realized that the evil, poisoned witch he had portrayed throughout my childhood was his own cruel creation; perhaps he knew the house of sand he had built for me was about to crumble into the tide. Who knows?

My grandfather once told me of a time when I went out to play with my cousins. I was only a little boy at the time: less than five years old. It was fall. Behind my grandfather's home, canyons cut into the red sands of McLoud. They were only about twenty feet deep, but they seemed cavernous to us kids. We had all gone down there to play and, after about an hour, all the kids returned home: all except me. Upon my grandfather's query, they told him they had hidden me in the canyon.

"Get down there and get him!" He demanded.

The canyons were covered in the colorful foliage of the season, and my cousins decided to play a little game with me. It was a game I knew well. They convinced me my mother was coming and I must hide in the leaves.

I instinctively dove to the ground as they helped to cover me with more fall color. Then as they left, I lay there in the cool dirt, covered in crisp fall leaves until they came back and told me the coast was clear.

Even today, my cousin, Jackie, recalls our uncle Everett—who wasn't much older than she—shouting to me that my mother was coming. It was winter; Jackie says I dove to the ground and tried to dig into the snow to cover myself. I was trained well.

My father may have chosen to plead the Fifth, but I was still waiting to hear from my mother. I knew there would be an abundance of answers from her, if only she would make that call or write that letter. All I could do was pray that she would want to know her son.

In the back of my mind I knew there was the chance she may have gotten upset with me, because I had not found her all those years. At thirty-three years of age, you would think I would have sone so—if that was my true desire.

One thing I soon discovered was that my mother would not call, nor would she write.

Chapter 8

Not the way you might expect to find her

A typical day in Houston: hot and humid with gulls wheeling in the thermals over the wide shipping channel. I was running errands, navigating the detours of what seemed a single mass of construction zones. To be fair, they did end, though upon completion they merely moved a block or two. Still, with my mother on my mind, a positive attitude prevailed as I arrived back home.

Evelyne obviously heard me pull in. When I opened the door, she was standing in the living room at the end of the foyer. Her eyes were wide and she wasn't smiling.

"Baby, I want you to sit down. I have something I need to tell you," she said, taking me by the hand.

Needless to say, I was scared. The way she was talking made me feel as if my world was about to collapse. We sat down on the sofa.

"Jack just called."

At first, I was confused. "Jack who?" I asked. Then I realized: *My mother's husband—Jack Stamper!*

"I knew this would happen when I was gone!" I shouted, jumping to my feet. "What did he say?"

"He said he got your letter and wanted to talk to you." I was dazed; I had come one step closer to my mother. Evelyne said he didn't leave a number, but would call again later. I was on tenterhooks and paced around the phone.

Later, as if by magic, the phone rang again. Though excited beyond belief, I was still apprehensive. Why didn't my mother call? My mind raced, thinking perhaps she died just a few days or weeks earlier. What else was I to think? Maybe Jack called just to tell me never to try and contact her again…

She hates you! I imagined him saying.

I answered the phone, and it was indeed Jack. It was beyond comprehension that I was speaking to the man who lives with my mother.

"Sorry if you can't hear me," he apologized in his country twang. "I'm callin' from a pay phone at the gas station next to the road."

"No problem!" I exclaimed, thinking: *are you kidding me? I would've listened on a string and two cans if I had to!*

As nice as he seemed on the phone, I was still worried. Why was *he* still calling? Where was my mother? There was a reason, and mercifully, Jack got straight to the point.

"Well, I need to tell ya. Your mom is probably not the way you might expect to find her."

She's alive! I thought.

"Oh yeah?" I said, feeling somewhat lame, except that I didn't know what else to say. Just how is a son supposed to find his mother after more than thirty years?

"Well, just wanted to let you know, because you may not want to have a relationship with her in the condition she's in," he said into the wake of my sinking heart.

I braced myself, head in hand with the phone pressed to my ear.

"Your mom looked for you for years. I know because I put her on a plane myself two or three times for her to go lookin' for ya. And once, she drove down to McLoud when we went to visit my mom and dad in McAlester. But your mom, after lookin' for you for years, and some other family problems goin' on, tried to kill herself back in seventy-three."

It seemed my mind was locked up and racing at the same time.

...don't you think if your momma wanted anything to do with you, she would've already found you?

But she was out there searching for me all that time—because she loved me.

"One night I guess she just had all she could take, and she took a bunch of prescription pills with some alcohol and tried to do herself in. So today, I suppose your mom is pretty much like a big kid. Pretty much what she does anymore is just watch TV all day."

The whole thing had become surreal. Just to know that my mother loved me was like being born again.

"Of course I want a relationship with her!"

"I was hopin' you were gonna say that."

"She's my mom, Jack."

"Well she'll be glad to see ya. I didn't show her your letter, because I didn't want her to get her hopes up. I'll let you read it to her when you get here."

Jack and I talked for a while about our past and how he drove up just after my father had taken off with me from the convenience store. He was pulling up to the house as my mother was running down the road, crying, waving her hands to stop him. She told him how my father had lied to her and taken off.

"We drove around for hours looking for your dad's car, but we never seen him."

Another bit of information he offered was that my father

knew the Stamper family. Not only had he been to their house, he had stayed there with my mother for a Jehovah's Witness Convention in September 1963. My father also knew where Bryan Mason, my grandfather, lived. He knew where the family lived in Arizona. He knew where Jack's parents lived, and had even told me that my mother "married a Jack Stamper or Standard, something like that." But, as ever, *he wasn't really sure.*

So who is the real conniver? I thought

As we ended our conversation, I made plans to fly up. And Jack made a forceful last remark: "Now I don't want you comin' up here gettin' her all upset because she didn't find you. She looked for you for a hell of a long time. I don't want any of that."

"That won't happen Jack," I promised.

I hung up the phone and smiled as I realized that in only a few days, I would see my mother again after more than three decades.

It was not until I was in the car and headed to the airport that I realized the magnitude of what was happening. I was coming to the end of my lifelong journey. Even at Hobby Airport, as Evelyne kissed me goodbye at the curb, a fog filled my senses. I felt a hundred emotions internalized and muted. Yet, at the same time, I wanted to scream to all those I encountered that *after more than thirty years, I had found my mother.*

The excitement ran through my veins like cold electricity. The whole journey that day was as if I was inside a snow globe. It seemed I was traveling in some sort of space warp. I could see everyone, but no-one knew I was there. I was carrying a special and perfect understanding of life and love and where it all lies, and all the people passing me by, sitting next to me, hadn't a clue the world was about to shift on its axis. Though I did not scream out, my insides were bubbling with an excited energy I had never felt before. I floated from car to check-in to terminal, and finally, onto the plane. Unable to hold this mammoth news inside, I imparted it to a select few. I told the girl at the ticket counter I was about to see my mother for the first time in decades. I told the woman sitting next to me on the plane my entire story of abduction, lies and mystery. She intently listened to stories of cult oppression and demonic possession. She held my hand and wished me well as our plane descended to the land down below. It is a land I know well: Oklahoma.

I rented a car and drove south on the Indian Nation Turnpike. With its giant median and four lanes carved through the countryside, it was worth the toll, having a higher speed limit and less traffic than the freeway. This was the first time I was really alone, and I slipped into a trance of sorts as I glided down the road.

On this lonely stretch of highway across the rolling hills of Eastern Oklahoma, it hit me. For a lifetime I had told my story. I had captivated many a friend and stranger with my story of kidnap and life on the run, of how I had searched and cried, then picked myself up and searched again. But it isn't just a story. *It is me.* I am that little boy looking through the back window of a speeding car, reaching out to the receding image of my mother with chubby toddler arms. I am the preschooler, the kindergartner, the grade-school boy who cried himself to sleep at night, quietly begging for his mother. It never was a story. *It was my life!* And my life, as I knew it, was about to come to an end. I had never concerned myself with what it would be like to actually find my mother, with what life would be like *after* the search was completed. It always seemed a mirage, a mysterious way of being.

Never in my life have I had so many emotions running through my body at once. I was excited because I was about to hold my mother in my arms. I was angry with my father for keeping me from her. I was nervous. I was happy. I was sad. I was scared; scared because I didn't know what to expect. *She's not the way you might expect to find her... Will she really know who I am?* Would I find my mother to be a mere shell of a woman? Jack told me she attempted suicide, and succeeded only in damaging her brain. How bad was it? Will she speak to me? Hold my hand? Will she be able to look into my eyes and say, "I love you, son?" Would she even realize she was my mother?

As the confusing possibilities raced through my mind, I even entertained the thought of turning around. I didn't know it was going to be like this, and I felt utterly overwhelmed. I had no idea that finding my mother would be such a sensation overload.

As I traveled closer, the emotions grew stronger and stronger. By the time I hit the last toll stop, I was drained. *This is it.*

Of course I tried to convince myself it was the beginning as well as the end of my journey: a new life with my mother! But I didn't know her and didn't know if she would even recognize me. Even if the past thirty years had been lonely, they were familiar and safe. *Better the devil you know,* as the saying goes. I know what to expect each morning as I wake.

But this—this is so much change all at once, and I'm not prepared...

And how can you be prepared, for God's sake? I was traveling to a mythical land armed only with stories told by its elders, who had left me with more nightmares than dreams.

But I was past the point of returning to an emotionally safe place. I was not about to turn tail and run. My mother was just over those hills; I was damned if I was to end my journey without her.

Coasting off the Turnpike, I headed toward McAlester: a quaint town, obviously bustling in its heyday. Today she's a sleepy grandmother with beautiful brick and stone buildings towering along Main Street. The majestic courthouse still serves up justice for the likes of Terry Nichols. Just a little farther on the left is the Grand International Temple Supreme Assembly Order of the Rainbow for Girls. And towering across the street is the First Christian Church where Reverend W. Mark Sexson wrote the original ceremony of initiation for Order of the Rainbow Girls.

I stopped at a florist and bought a dozen red roses. I told my story as I paid for the flowers; the woman at the counter cried and embraced me as I left. I thought about when I was in elementary school and I stopped and picked Dandelions from the yard and gave them to Jo, my stepmother. Such a simple and easy task, and yet, here I am in my mid-thirties, and for the first time in my life I'm picking flowers for my mother. I had lost so much. My mother had lost even more. She never saw me off to my first day of school, helped me with my homework, or encouraged me in my dreams. I was unable to hold her tight and tease her because I had grown taller. She never knew my first love. Nor was she there to console me after my first heartbreak. I never got to ask her *what do you think of Betty?* or *How about Sally?* She was not there to hold my daughter—her first grandbaby—when she was born. She wasn't allowed to give me the love and tenderness I craved. She wasn't there. And I wasn't there. And all this was because of one man and his fanatical self-righteous beliefs, and because of his selfishness. My mother and I lost our lives. We lost our happiness as it could have been. We lost our rights as mother and son. We both had walked the earth, searching, hoping one day to hold one another. Now that day had come. And I was going to give my mother flowers.

After making my way through McAlester with Jack's directions, I easily managed to get lost. Up ahead, the red awning of one of the few gas stations came into view. I pulled into the white gravel lot and spotted a public phone.

Inside the small tin building, the smell of fried chicken and corndogs wafted about. The attendant's backwoods reply to my request for change took me back to the summers I had spent with my cousins in McLoud and Webber Falls, only ninety miles away. Could she have lived not even two hours away all those summers I'd spent in Oklahoma? The cowbell on the door clanked as I swung it shut and marched across the blinding gravel. I called Jack from the phone booth at the edge of the road.

The number he gave me was for his mother, Lillie, who lived next door. Over the passing tractor trailers, not thirty feet from the phone, I told him the name of the gas station where I had taken refuge.

Five minutes later, he arrived in a green and white '72 Ford pickup, rattling across the gravel next to my car. The engine died, and out bounced Jack. I just stood there as he walked over, a barrel-chested, red-haired man in overalls, with no t-shirt. His possum grin deepened the lines in his weathered face.

"Bryan?" He asked.

"That's me." I extended my hand in greeting.

This teddy bear of a man shook my hand and gave me a hug. He seemed as excited as I was, and quickly shot back to his truck.

"C'mon. I'll get ya to the house. Your momma's waitin' for ya."

I just shook the hand of my mother's husband. I thought as I jumped into my car. *What a sensation!*

Pulling onto the highway, I followed him the short distance to the dirt road. Jack's truck billowed up a cloud of dust as we passed one small ranch or farm after another. Pulling back from his wake, grey squirrels shot across the road and up the trees, barking as I passed. Eventually, the dust settled as I saw his old truck turn in through a cyclone gate. I slowed the dusty car, eased through the gate behind him, and parked.

Their house was a simple one, which he said he built himself back in '82. Five or six dogs crowded around the car to get a look at the city boy as raucous guinea hens cackled their way clear.

We made small talk about how great the weather was for the drive as we walked to the door. But my thoughts were not in the sun. This day, these twenty simple steps were all that stood between me and my mother. I didn't have to live without her any longer.

He swung the door open and stood there holding the screen, raising his arm to show me the way.

"Go ahead on," He smiled.

I grasped my roses tight, passed over the threshold, and entered the room.

There, in the corner, was my Holy Grail: my mother. She sat there with her long, silver Cherokee ponytail flowing over her shoulder. Rosy lipstick and face powder graced her face, though it obviously was applied by Jack. Rocking back and forth, looking up at me, then back to the floor, and again at me, she was as nervous as I. So there she was, this silver-haired lady, having waited over thirty years to see her child, to hold the son she carried inside her only to have him ripped away.

I quickly went to her and put one arm around her as I set the roses on the floor. Then, as I put my arms around her, we both began crying.

"My boy, come back to me! My boy, come back to me!" She cried, over and over.

Holding the back of her head, I pressed our cheeks together as our tears mingled.

"I'm back, Mom."

Her cries filled the room as Jack raised her arms around me, as she wasn't able to do this on her own. After so many years, of searching and begging my father to let her see me, she finally had her son in her arms. And I had my mother. No more guessing, searching, crying at night. No more horrible tales of demonic possession; no more mind control.

"You're not gonna leave me are ya, boy, huh? You're not gonna leave me again are ya?" She pleaded, through her tears.

"No mom. I'm not going to leave you. Not ever again. I promise."

I knelt and embraced her as she sat in her chair, crying, wiping her tears, holding on. I didn't want to let go. I wanted to be that little boy again sitting in her lap, pressed against her warmth. I wanted to go back to before that time: before the day we didn't even get to say goodbye. I just wanted my mother.

After we dried out and things settled down, I pulled a chair from the kitchen and sat next to her. Then, for the first time in over thirty years, I held my mother's hand.

"Get his clothes Jack, get his clothes," she said over and

over until Jack acknowledged her.

"Okay, okay. I'll get his clothes." I was a little confused as Jack headed out of the living room. The creaking of a door or two filled the room, a few bumps and a slide across a wall. Confused, I looked at my mother.

"I got your clothes boy, I got your clothes," she told me.

Soon he returned with a clear plastic blanket-bag, with a zipper that ran across three sides. It contained no blanket, but I could see it was filled with different colored fabric.

"That's yours son. It's yours," my mother proudly announced.

I took the bag, and pulled the zipper. The stagnant odor of old mothballs pierced my senses, and I fell speechless as I pulled out *my clothes*. They were my old baby clothes: over thirty years old. I held one jumper, putting the feet to the floor, and it barely reached my knees. There was a dark brown "little man" suit, complete with a tan "little man" shirt. It even had a matching clip-on tie.

"Your momma kept those. I don't know how many years. After a while, she figured you wasn't comin' back. Several times she wanted to give 'em away to friends. But I always told her, 'One day he's gonna walk through that door and you're gonna kick yourself in the butt for gettin' rid of 'em.'"

All those years she had been looking for me, she'd kept my clothes for my return. She was waiting for me. I was very happy, to say the least, that Jack had told her to keep them.

"Thanks so much, Mom." I told her with a hug.

"You're welcome," She replied, proudly.

After examining the tiny outfits, she began speaking of letters and pictures. It took a few tries, but she finally heaved herself up from her chair. She began the trip across the living room to her bedroom, but only after picking up her trash can, of course. She goes nowhere without the security of her little trash can. After leading me to her bedroom, she stood in front of her dresser and directed me to one drawer after another. There were so many pictures and letters that I was pulling them from everywhere. Waddling back to her chair, she sat back down and we flipped through the letters, some dated as far back as 1955.

Later, as we went through the pictures, I asked the names of those I should have known and loved: relatives I never met. There was my grandmother and grandfather, my aunt, cousins, great grandparents, and great uncles and aunts. There were even great, great grandparents. It was endless. *What a crime, I thought. This huge family, generations of my family, and I knew none of them.*

Then I saw a small photo of a beautiful woman. I couldn't help but stare. My eyes welled up and my heart pounded. I recognized a vibrant, twenty-something woman.

"That's me," my mother giggled. "That's me right there."

"Yes it is," I replied.

How wonderful it could have been to have known my own mother. To laugh with her, and know what would set her off. It makes me weak inside to know how much we lost. Our true lives were stolen, and nothing on the face of the earth can ever get that back for us. I felt sad and angry at the same time: that a man who should have had undying love for me, killed the life my mother and I should have had.

I replaced her picture in the stack and continued through the old memories as she called out their names. Time and again, she'd call Jack over to check her memory.

Flipping through likenesses of several children, she called out, "There you are!"

On a manicured lawn with a palm tree in the background,

a child attempted to push a lawnmower bigger than him. He was a baby really: about eighteen months old, sporting a cloth diaper. It was such an odd feeling to see myself in the picture she had taken, fighting with that 1960s lawnmower, which I'm sure weighed a ton. Then another one popped up. In it were several kids on a sofa with what looked like their mother. And then another.

"I must be at least two there," I told her, but it was foreign: a life of which I had no recollection and to which I had no connection. But I could see it was me and I looked happy. Yet this was a picture of me taken by the woman who allegedly "threw" me "ten feet across the room." The evil-to-the-core, demonic, possessed woman? My father had me convinced for years—and expected my praise for his heroism!

The next photo caught me by surprise. I recognized myself again, this time standing by a table topped with a silver tray. I knew that picture.

How did she get this?

Then it hit me. The letter she wrote in June 1972, just a year before she attempted suicide: *Thank you very-very much for the pictures... I hope that some day you'll find it in your heart to let me see him...*

What a travesty. What a crime.

My stepsister, Kathy, tells me it was taken at our home in Indiana, where we lived after my father wed her mother. He had moved us across the river from Louisville, Kentucky, to keep me hidden.

After reading a few of the letters, looking at many pictures and taking a few of my own, Jack appeared behind me.

"Here," is all he said, as he handed me one last letter. "I told ya I didn't read it to her. Thought you might want to."

I recognized the certified letter. I didn't put my name on

the return address because I was afraid she wouldn't open it if she knew it was from me.

"I'm gonna feed the animals." He walked through the kitchen and out to the back yard.

I took the last letter of our very first day together, and I read aloud my nervous, scribbled, words, written an eternity ago.

Dear Angie,

Well it's taken me 15 years, but I finally found you. Before I continue this letter, I want you to know that I realize not all reunions are great. Sometimes coming together just is not for every person. So I will let you know now that I will not try to contact you again. Not unless you contact me first. I pray you do.

I first tried to find you when I was 18. I was getting married. Dad called around and found some people who knew you. They said you were dead. Convenient for Dad I suppose. I never really believed it. I suppose it just didn't feel right. I'm glad I went with my feelings. Through my searches I did find that your mother was buried in the Forrest Lawn Funeral home in Glendale. They told me she is in a double plot but no-one was with her. That left me wondering about Bryan, if he was still around.

I hope you are doing well. I can truly say that I have never been so happy in my life as I am now. The marriage I told you about only lasted about 5 years. But what can you expect when you marry so young. This union did bring me a wonderful daughter though. Her name is Anna Monique, she is 12. I have a beautiful *girlfriend from France, Evelyne. We are actually common law married. It's a good thing I suppose. Dad & his wife Jo would not have anything to do with me otherwise. I am not one of the Jehovah's Witnesses any more. Evelyne and I are more concerned about the spirituality of the person inside than the beliefs by which one is led.*

There is no way to convey 30 years in a letter. Growing up as a child who didn't belong into a young man searching for someone just to love him; getting married twice and ending up with a brain injury. I've been to Hell and back and I feel like I cheated the devil. It took me 33 years to find happiness. But now I have it and I know how to keep it. Evelyne and I have been together 13 months. She only just now understands why I can't discuss my childhood.

I don't mean to get so negative, but I think a great tragedy in life is living in the shadows of the decisions that others make.

I'm not talking about you. After the last time you saw me. Dad moved from place to place. I lived in 5 different states before I even started the first grade. Odd to me was the fact that he never even thought that I would want or need to know my own mother. But I will tell you this, I lay no blame on anyone. I make no judgments! We all make mistakes in our own life. God knows I've made more than my share.

I've cried for you, I've longed for you, I've searched for you. You, mom. You are the last event in my life that I need closure on. Actually, seeing you or even just seeing your handwriting would not be a closure, it would be an opening. An opening of bright light in this

dark room that I've been in for 33 years.
Please contact me. I love you. What man could not
love his own mother?

Your Son,
Bryan

We both cried through the entire letter. I was overjoyed that she didn't throw my letter in the trash. How wonderful it felt just to sit next to my mother and hold her hand!

As you can imagine, stories abounded over the next few days. My mother, in spite of her severe brain damage, remembers an amazing number of past events and names. At Jack's request, she even states the names of certain therapists who worked with her after her attempted suicide. Jack also has his own stories to add to those my mother told him before she hurt herself.

The letters were amazing to read, and it was a delight to see the pictures and hear the stories of my own life and the family I never knew. Jack told me of times when he and my mother were friends and she would want to go here and there.

"No. We're not goin' anywhere he can't go," he would tell her.

"There were times when I'd just take off with you and go visit a friend or something. You'd just stand in the seat next to me, and we'd have a ball," Jack laughed.

It was so odd, to stare into his warm eyes, and still have no recollection of him. I asked if he'd ever known my mother to be short with me as a child, or perhaps even outright mean.

"No, I don't. The only thing I remember bad happenin' to you, was one time we went to the Colorado River. You had really bad diaper rash, so we let you run around butt naked the whole time, so you'd dry up." He laughed at this memory.

The smile washed from my face as I recalled my father saying, "I've seen your own momma say, 'I wish I'd never had this kid!' and then throw you ten feet across the room onto the bed!" It sounded plausible at an early age, but after hearing from Jack and later from Lillie, his mother, about how my mother searched and grieved for me, it no longer made sense.

"For years your mother said, 'If my boy loves me, why don't he come find me,'" Jack said.

Things gradually became clearer, even though in the middle of the situation I was still unable to sort things out completely. I did know this much: my mother wrote her pleading letter in '72, begging to see me. She traveled several times to search for me and, yes, to take me back to California.

What became more and more evident was the role of the Jehovah's Witness philosophy. My father was a servant, an elder, in the Organization, for decades. All the while he was teaching me that my mother was demonized and no less than a whore, having allowed "some guy" to rape her with impunity.

"For years the Witnesses would come around knocking on the door wanting to sell their magazines," Jack remembered. "I'd tell 'em about you and what your dad did. And every time I asked them to help your momma find you. And they'd throw their hands up: 'Oh no! We can't do that. We don't get involved in that stuff.'"

What Jack didn't understand was a closely held doctrine of the Witnesses, called *Theocratic Warfare*, wherein believers are taught that it is appropriate to withhold the truth from "people who are not entitled to it."

This is especially true of child custody cases in our own courts.

Jack was telling these people that a person within their own ranks was an abductor. But they didn't care. All they knew was that the woman inside the house was *not a Witness*, and they were not going to help a child find his *worldly* mother.

Later that same day my mother was sitting in her chair, sobbing.

"What's wrong mom? Your son's here!" I smiled and tried to console her.

And what she said resonated all the way back to Houston.

"Your daddy hired two men to rape me!" She said, as the tears cascaded down her cheeks.

The hair on my neck stood on end. This new twist was a ton of bricks, or more aptly, a knife through my back. I hesitated, and gathered my thoughts.

"I know Mom, I'm sorry." I told her.

I put my arms around her and held on as she cried. Could my dad have done that? He was a leader in several congregations for years, counseling others on their marriage problems, guiding and encouraging them to be "closer to God."

I could have attributed this story to my mother trying to get back at my father, but for one very incriminating point: my father had changed his version of events. How can you say your wife "bragged" that she "let the guy rape her," then later say you're not sure if she was raped or had sex?

More importantly, what kind of man would *hire someone to rape his own wife?* Not to mention hiring two of his own relatives! I have to admit that it seemed implausible. But it still bore an uncanny ring of truth.

I remembered him saying, "I've seen her stand there, bold face lyin', and be cryin' the whole time."

Could she have been trying to hide the humiliation? Perhaps she was trying to turn me against my father. I decided to maintain that I judged no-one and try to avoid being caught in the middle.

As the visit continued, my head whirled with images, stories, and hope. I took pictures of our heartfelt reunion as we laughed and cried over shared meals and stories. I spent time with Jack's mother, Lillie, a tiny woman, nearing eighty, a frail shell of the woman she once was. Having been my baby-sitter, her sharp memory carried even more information about my life with my mother.

"I told her to get a divorce," she related in her ancient voice. "I told her Freddie was gonna take you if she didn't get a divorce. 'He won't do that,' she told me. But he sure did it."

"Were you there when it happened?" I asked.

"Yeah. I was there. I told her to leave you with me. But she said no. She said Freddie gave her the keys to his car and it was okay."

My mother was so young. At that time she was only nineteen and my father almost thirty. No doubt he used his age and maturity to control any situation concerning her.

My father had made so many claims justifying his actions; I had to ask Lillie to confirm the truth of anything he said.

"Did you tell my father I'd be better off with him than my mother?" I asked her.

"Yeah—I did," She said, remorsefully. "I think I did it just because of the difference in the way we was raised. I wish I could a-raised ya! You was a cute little boy…"

Lillie left me a little confused. She told my mother to get a divorce because she was sure my father will take me away. But at the same time, she tells him I'd be better off with him. The fact that Lillie was born in the twenties may have influenced her thinking about the way my mother should have raised me. Unfortunately, Lillie has since passed on and we will never know her true intentions or ideas.

Though this journey had ended, a new one was just over the horizon. It seemed that, as soon as I arrived, I was packing to leave. We said our farewells, my luggage in hand, but it was evident my mother was upset. She had just had her son come back into her life for a mere four days after more than thirty years. She was sure I would never return.

"I'm coming back, Mom. I promise." I assured her.

It was difficult for me as well. Having just found her I wanted her in my life. But she lived so far away. I wiped her tears, kissed her goodbye, and left, knowing at last where my mother spent her days and that she truly did love me.

Chapter 9

You're not gonna pin that one on me

I was on sensory and emotional overload, having taken in so much information and experienced so much drama. I began to understand what I had really lost. My upbringing as a Jehovah's Witness did not allow me to face those feelings, that sense of loss. Witnesses are trained to avoid the *World and her disgusting things*.

My mother, according to the Witness viewpoint, was part of the world that God would soon destroy. I was trained to feel nothing—to repress my natural desire to be with her—for fear of falling into her abyss of debauchery. I was able to truly feel the loss when I broke away from the Watchtower. Now, having found her, I was flooded with the pent-up emotions of a lifetime.

I was numb during the drive back to Tulsa and the flight to Houston. My mind swam through the deluge of information I had received in those few days. I wasn't able to process much at all, although I began writing notes: trying to sort things out. I immediately began to compare what my father had told me with what my mother and Jack had said; checking dates from both sources and from the letters. I was glad to return to the security of my home.

Evelyne was anxious to hear how everything went. Of course, the first thing I wanted was to get the photographs to the lab for developing. Then I wanted to speak to my father.

Within a week, Jo called and said Kathy and Carrie were coming over for dinner and wondered if we would like to visit as well. This didn't happen very often and actually I was really glad of the invitation.

"Yeah. Sounds great," I told her.

I knew everyone would be interested to hear my experience and see the photos, including my father.

As usual, I was anxious. My first wife once told me how nervous I seemed around my father and stepmother. She was right; I have always been uncomfortable around them, sometimes to the point where I don't know what to say. Only in the last few years have I begun to understand why I let them affect me that way.

Evelyne and I were the last to arrive. I scanned the room to see if maybe Jo had displayed a picture or two more of me or Anna, at least to make me feel a little more at home. I should have known better.

Before we even sat down, the topic of conversation was my mother; rightly so. I started by explaining how she had searched for me for years, then, giving up, had attempted suicide. Immediately, I was transported into an old black and white James Cagney film. My father started up as if I'd just insulted him.

"You're not gonna pin that one on me!" He growled.

I didn't hesitate.

"Well I'd say you certainly contributed to it. Wouldn't you?"

Jo quickly interjected with how happy she was that I finally found my mother after all these years, as if she had been rooting for me all along. To be honest, I have no doubt it crossed Jo's mind to have me live with my mother. Too bad she couldn't have talked that bit of sense into her husband.

Dad quickly left to make himself another drink as we sat around the dining table and passed the pictures around. And yes, my father did gaze at the photos. I'd like to have been able to pick his brain and see what he was really thinking.

The tense dinner was soon over and on our way home, Evelyne and I discussed my father's agitation. His changing stories, obvious lies, sleeplessness, and denial of wrongdoing all prompted me to scrutinize any accusation he made or position he took.

Now that my mother was back in my life, I did feel more whole. And that healing has lightened my spirit. The bond between mother and son is more than tender kisses and bear hugs. The internal loss she suffered must have smothered her spirit to the point of physical illness. The pain heaped upon her by my father like coal into a furnace drove her to the point of giving up on life. He may not have provided the gun, but I'd certainly say he bought her a bullet or two.

My great journey has been completed; I did find my mother and it was *almost* a perfect story. The tragic path we followed, set out for us by my father, was not only emotionally destructive, but truly life changing for all involved.

I think back to his irritation, disappointment and disgust with me. Does he not understand that he created me? My personality has been molded by his callous actions and lack of love. Yet he blames me and my mother for his lack of sleep. Does he not understand the years we lost?

Now, another journey lay before me: a journey to discover my true past, my father's true actions, and my mother's life. My fear of the truth kept curiosity at bay for a time. But after a few years, desire for the truth would not let me rest, even though I knew I would have to pursue it into dark and forbidden places.

If my mother's accusations were true, my father certainly would have been more diabolical than he could ever had made her out to be. Can you imagine a man sitting in his living room, holding his seven-month-old child on the sofa, gazing into that child's eyes, knowing that his wife is being subdued and perhaps dragged through woods or shoved into a car? Imagine: the baby cries as he moves to the kitchen to warm a bottle. As he glances at the clock, he's sure she's being raped by two men she once trusted, two men he sent out: his own relatives.

I knew I didn't want to go there. At the same time there were just too many questions and facts staring me in the face.

And what of my mother? Do those without justice not deserve it? Was thirty years too long to wait to resurrect the putrid skeletons of my father's house? When you know someone is hurt, how can you not follow the trail of blood?

Then again, perhaps my mother was simply "bold-face lyin'" as the tears streamed down her face.

Chapter 10

I hope you two are happy together

The emotional highs and lows weaving through my life have brought tears of joy, cries of abandonment, elated sensations of love, and heartbreaking loss. Looking back on my jagged path, having written these words, I am amazed that I still walk the earth. And for that I give thanks for the wellspring of inner strength in my soul, for it has sustained me even when I did not know of it, or believed it was spent.

The desire for true love, I like to believe, has set me back on my feet more than once, to fight again. Through the centuries many men have died for the sake of love; whether for the honor of a beautiful maiden or the life of an innocent child. Perhaps this same devotion to love has forced me to live for that same maiden and child. Possibly my path was set out before I began, and I am no more than a bewildered spectator experiencing my predestined fate. Somewhere, in the very breath of us all is the truth.

Truth, though, is too often relative, a unique combination of each of us with our surroundings. What is normal is simply that with which we are familiar. As a young man I knew without doubt, and preached zealously, that God would cleanse this wicked earth before the year two thousand. That was reality for me as it was taught in my life. But, at times what we observe is not the truth. It is the truth, not our perception of it, that will set us free.

Finding and reuniting with my mother was my truth. In an effort to be *normal,* I considered my parents' accusations against one another to be a tug-o'-war over me; my abduction was a game of "he said, she said." I decided at first to leave it at that; I could not bring back my mother's health and had no power to calm my father's anger.

I took this approach for some time, as it also seemed the healthiest option for my own emotional wellbeing. After all, I had completed an unbelievable, journey and after more than thirty years, regained my forbidden mother. I had great hope that my new peace would be the mystical ointment with which to heal my pain. Normality was my greatest desire. Satisfaction of self and a feeling of wholeness, I prayed, would direct my new existence.

But having made this decision, I could not find rest. Once the void of my mother's absence was filled, another vacuum revealed itself. Unquenchable desire for the complete truth grew exponentially and I was unable to quail the doubts that nagged my mind.

Before long my father cut off all communication with me and my family, after discovering I had attended the Unity Church of Houston instead of his Kingdom Hall of Jehovah's Witnesses.

The Watchtower has decreed for decades that even family members should be treated as outcasts if they stop believing and practicing in the way prescribed in their literature. It's no different from being disfellowshipped for a gross sin.

I had one final phone conversation with my father. "You're an apostate. I can't associate with you any more," he declared.

Quite honestly, I didn't care. He was evading my questions concerning my mother and we really didn't have any sort of relationship to lose. No sad farewells were in order.

"Do what you have to do," I curtly replied. I can be as stubborn as any McGlothin.

"Well, I hope you two are happy together" were his last words.

From the moment I found my mother up to that last conversation, my father seemed genuinely angry. But I had detected something else. His refusing to speak about my mother, saying he had "lost two days' sleep," along with the photos and documents of which he divested himself, indicated that there was something else behind his cutting communication. I sensed he knew I would soon discover the truth I so deeply desired, the truth of which he had not given me the privilege before, and that, perhaps, he hoped I would never find. I don't think he looked forward to the tough questions he knew would follow once I arrived at this truth.

As days, weeks, and months elapsed, and I spent additional time with my mother and Jack, I heard even more of the other side of the story. I read and re-read the letters my mother had kept and discovered that, for years, she had truly searched for me. She really did love me, and still does. Jack revealed many stories she told him before giving up on her own life: stories even I cannot put to paper. Over time, it started eating at me; especially the account of rape, told by both my mother and father. Were it not for my father's changing story, I might not have been so hungry for answers. But his contradictions had left me questioning everything he had told me. I began to feed my hunger and skepticism with research.

Using all tools at my disposal, I traveled virtually coast to coast, researching court documents and searching for my lost family. I found aunts and an uncle, along with several cousins. I was told stories by persons who hadn't spoken to each other in decades, yet their accounts of events were similar.

Many times I was moved as I heard stories of a wonderful woman.

"Your mother was a light in my life," a second cousin said.

"After your father took you, she was never the same," her aunt told me.

"She loved you so much…"

"She was a great mom…"

"It destroyed her…"

The experiences related to me were far from the stories of the abusive, demonic libertine my father had spoon-fed me for decades.

I spent many hours in several courthouses discovering an arrest warrant, multiple divorce filings, a "Petition for Separate Maintenance," and a restraining order. I searched through microfiche of old newspapers in libraries. Even at home, the internet proved an invaluable tool.

My search led me so far and deep into a labyrinth of tales and half-truths that I could not avoid speaking with one of the men that my father claimed had raped my mother. I went much farther than I intended, but the quest for truth became as a drug. There was no quenching my desire for the facts.

Now, after close to eight years of research, I have more of the truth than I ever wanted.

Chapter 11

Let him go or I'm gonna shoot!

Born in Tucson, Arizona, my mother, Angie Lenora Mason, lived a gypsy's life with her older sister Sherry Irene, thanks to their father, Bryan, whose name I bear. Bryan was a WWII Air force Veteran who came from a long line of Cherokee blood.

Lola Mae, their mother, a descendant of the Isle of Jersey Poindexters, was the only constant force in their little lives.

Bryan and Lola's relationship was a toxic one, battered by several separations and a divorce, after which they reconciled until Lola's death. It wasn't an easy life for my mother and her sister; they endured much along with their mother.

As a family, they constantly moved between Tucson, Arizona, Baldwin Park, California, and Ada, Oklahoma. The only certainty in their life was change: change and conflict. Bryan, when drunk, was violently abusive.

My mother and her sister, when still very young, were once forced to sit on the sofa and watch their father beat their mother with a broom handle until she passed out.

"And when she'd come to, he'd beat her again," my aunt said.

In that same little travel trailer, Sherry told me, their father, my grandfather, beat her and her sister without mercy.

"Bruises on our little faces..." she recalled; "...he made

us both sit on the sofa, and he took a picture of us." The pain was evident on her face.

Vera, my great-aunt, told of one incident during the same period when Bryan—drunk—began beating my mother and her sister again. My grandmother Lola, as usual, jumped between her husband and children and shouted to the little girls, "Run to Daddo's and tell him not to let Daddy have you!"

Sherry and my mother ran to their grandfather's trailer through the high grass. Vera, pregnant with her first child, was with her parents. She remembers that day vividly.

They lived in the foothills of Tucson, Arizona; Lola and her sister Vera lived with their families on adjacent two-and-a-half-acre lots. Their mother and father, Angie Leslie and George Washington Turner had moved their travel trailer onto Vera and her husband's property.

Once they arrived at their grandparents', they told their Grandfather how his son-in-law had drained another bottle.

"Sit on the sofa. I won't let him have ya," George assured his granddaughters.

Soon after the little girls arrived, Lola Mae appeared at her parents' trailer, disheveled and breathless, saying that Bryan was on his way.

True to her word, Bryan soon arrived and demanded his children.

"I'm not gonna do that, Bryan. You need to get home and sober up," George insisted.

"You give me my kids or I'm gonna get my gun!" My grandfather threatened.

"You get your gun," was the determined reply.

Bryan wobbled to his car and drove the short distance home. George, concerned for everyone in the house, loaded

his World War I Army issue rifle, propped it behind the front
door, and waited.

Bryan returned, as promised, with his own rifle. George,
almost seventy years old, stood firm in the doorway as Bryan
approached. My grandfather, rifle in hand, cursed his father-
in-law. George, instinctively, lunged for him. Bryan, almost
fifty years George's junior, met him halfway. They both hit the
dirt, grappling for Bryan's gun. Struggling to their feet, both
men got a firm hand on the barrel of the rifle and began slug-
ging each other, fist to face, over and over again. Vera, fearing
for her father's life, grabbed his rifle from behind the door and
ran to the brawl. Lola Mae and her mother, Angie Leslie, were
screaming and crying as a cloud of blinding dust billowed
about the mayhem. The men tussled in the sand, pummeling
each other's faces, struggling over the weapon. My mother and
her sister, tiny children, were terrified. Vera thrust the barrel
of her father's rifle hard against my grandfather's back.

"Let my dad go, Bryan!" Vera shouted. "Let him go or I'm
gonna shoot!"

Bryan began swinging his father-in-law about, attempting
to put George between himself and the rifle. But Vera dog-
gedly followed Bryan round and round, jabbing and thrusting
the weapon at her brother-in-law's back.

"Let him go, Bryan!" She shouted again.

With women and girls yelling and screaming, fists flying,
and weapons in the mix, the situation seemed set to be
resolved in the worst possible way, but Vera, with that rifle at
the ready, was concerned solely with protecting her father.

At a moment of impasse, as Vera prepared to do the
unthinkable, a huge hand seized the rifle from her hands and
flung the weapon to the sky in a single motion. She swung
around in a cloud of dust and venom to face her husband,

Alvin Travers. He had heard the commotion and came running to the family's aid. Al wrestled the barrel of Bryan's rifle from the brawling men as they neared fatigue.

"Go home, Bryan." Al told my grandfather in a calm voice.

Bryan loosed his grip on his father-in-law and meekly returned to his car.

"Don't come back until you've sobered up!" Vera shouted. My grandfather drove home and did what he was told; he didn't return to his in-laws' home for at least a week.

Lola was seen many times with bruises about her body and face. My mother and her sister witnessed this for years and it obviously scarred them. But even though Lola Mae was probably codependent and lacking self esteem as a result of her husband's physical, mental and verbal abuse, it does take more than one to make a fight, as one particular story illustrates.

Not long after Lola and Bryan married, they planned a dinner for her parents and younger sisters, Vera and Georgia Lee. As afternoon faded into evening and dinner had been ready for some time, Bryan still had not returned home.

"Why don't we go ahead and get started while it's warm? I'll heat some up for Bryan when he gets here," Lola suggested.

Her parents agreed and everyone sat around the table to have dinner without Bryan. They enjoyed an evening of family company and good food. Then, as the table was being cleared, Bryan arrived home.

An argument soon broke out and escalated between Lola and Bryan. Enraged and yelling, they began to smash plates, cups, and saucers against the walls and floor. Bryan stretched his arm across the half-cleaned table and sent the remaining food and dishes clattering to the floor. By this time, Lola's parents had escaped to the yard as they didn't believe in interfering with their children's lives. Lola's younger sisters, Vera and Georgia Lee, remained in the trailer and watched with wide eyes.

Once they had exhausted the supply of dishes on the table and countertops, they began unloading the cabinets. Only when every dish was reduced to smithereens did they stop fighting.

That day, Lola was equally responsible for the violence. Perhaps it was a proving ground for later combat. Regardless, the next day, Bryan returned home after work with a box of new dishes.

This was their pattern for many years. Even when my mother was fourteen, her father, drunk and riled over something, once cornered her in the kitchen.

As he drew back his hand to strike her, Lola Mae grabbed an iron skillet. She ran up behind Bryan, raised the hefty pan over her head poised to strike him with it just as Bryan passed out, fortunately for him, and fell to the floor.

This was the environment in which my mother learned about love and life; one in which fear, hate, and chaos were ever-lurking demons.

In a letter dated February 13th 1955, my grandmother writes my grandfather:

> *After you left I didn't have anyone to take care of the kids, so I had to quit my job...*

Angie Lenora, my mother, was almost eight years old, and my grandfather was in Marana, Arizona where his parents, Wilton and Nora, lived. Lola continues by telling him that she applied for state aid:

> *But before they would help me I had to sign some papers that I was willing for them to pick you up if necessary.*

A few days later, on February 17th, Lola Mae writes my grandfather again, having received a letter from him immediately after her first letter.

> *Angie Lenora kept me up after midnight last night crying to see you. Sherry didn't cry. She just set up wide eyed and was trying to figure out some way to save enough money to get something to send you. They aren't interested in school anymore or anything for that matter. They just keep saying that they don't have a daddy.*

She continues:

> *You can write awfully sweet letters not to be able to say anything sweet when you're home. Yes I get awfully lonesome myself and the kids sure make things hard for me too. But they (people) say time changes everything. Sometime I wonder. Well life is hard, the very best a body can do, and when they let wine, women, & song, & crime get the best of them, it don't just hurt them, it hurts every one they come in contact with. It seems there are more broken homes & heart break over those things. When little innocent children have to suffer is the worst part of it. God only knows how I've suffered while I lived with you. And it looks like my*

suffering is just beginning. I know I have every right in the world to hate you. But I can't say I do & tell the truth. There's not a better man in the world then you are when you want to be. But I guess I'm not the woman to bring out the best in you. I never felt secure with you as long as we were married. I felt I had to be the strong one because of your weakness for drink. When everything in me cried out for someone to lean on.

My grandmother, like many abused wives, took the fault upon herself: *I guess I'm not the woman to bring out the best in you.* She was a beaten woman, suffering by then from emphysema. When Bryan moved her and Sherry back to Southern California, her health was at its worst. He chose to live in a trailer park right on the Santa Monica freeway. It seems he was unaware of the smog from the constant traffic within yards of their home.

Lola Mae's complaints to my mother began as early as January 21st 1964 a few months before I was born. She writes:

I'm sure tired living in this [dungeon] by the freeway.

She tells my mother more as her health worsens, writing to her on February, 5th 1964:

I hate this court we are in. Seems like we are down in a hole. And the noise from the freeway is enough to drive one mad not to even mention the fumes from so many cars. An ideal place for someone who has asthma, emphasema & ulcers. Especially if they don't want to live long.

Then on March 19th 1964, she writes:

If I just had some good air to breathe—These fumes from the freeway is enough to kill a well person.

Less than two months later, my grandmother was dead.

About nine months before Lola's death, my mother had already left her parents' home, had been married to my father for three months, and was pregnant with me. The new couple's home was in McLoud, Oklahoma, while Angie's sister and parents had moved back to Baldwin Park, California, a separation that caused my mother deep distress.

On September 22nd 1963, my Aunt Sherry writes my mother:

I thought I'd write to let you know that mom had a severe attack of asthma and we liked to not got her to the hospital in time. She turned as black as any black I've ever seen. But don't worry I'll take care of her. If she gets any worse I'll take her to the doctor."

Though Sherry was the older sister, she was only nineteen, and seemed to be carrying the burden of the family. She continues:

I never seen anyone like Dad in my whole life. He was supposed to see this guy for a job and he didn't go that day so I got after him the next day and he called the man and was supposed to see him the next day but he didn't and he never called either. He just drinks wine as fast as he can buy it. He just stays here on Dub and Shug, I never seen anything to come down to his level. He piles in on one relative after another, just makes the rounds."

George Washington Turner Jr., nicknamed "Dub," was Lola Mae's brother; Shug was his wife. Being my grandmother's family, of course, Dub wanted to help his little sister, and my grandfather was only too happy to accept the offer. Sherry continues her letter:

She got so bad when we rushed her to the hospital that the doctor asked if she wanted to see her minister. I'm taking as good care of her as I can. Dad could help if he would stay home instead of stay gone and getting drunk. Instead of trying to take care of mom, Dad shows his _____.

This is the life my mother endured. Her father turned to the bottle even as her mother was dying before his eyes.

This chaotic background may have been why she said yes to my father when he asked her to be his wife. Her mother, Lola Mae, was excited that a young servant in the Jehovah's Witness Organization was asking for her daughter in marriage. On March 20th 1964, my grandmother writes my mother, who is seventeen and seven months pregnant with me:

I know Fred is good to you and looks out for your spiritual interests. I had him pretty well sized up before you married him.

I'm sure she wanted her daughter out of the house as desperately as my mother wanted out herself.

I read the heartfelt letters and heard the disturbing stories of my grandfather and I rejected even the thought of searching for him. He had not seen my mother in decades and had not called in over ten years. He left my mother crying and heartbroken by calling to say he was stopping by while on vacation, and then neither arrived nor called back. I saw no need to have him in my life.

But as I began to discover more family throughout the country and heard their stories, I began to soften towards him. *Perhaps I should hear his side,* I thought.

Jack told me Bryan's last phone call to my mother had been to say that his second wife, Belen, had died. He and Belen were together for over twenty years, and I hoped that she might have weaned him from his bottle. For good or bad, I was going to dig deeper into my, dark, family closet.

I had no idea what to expect even if I could locate this man with his dark history. Not one family member I spoke with could utter a kind word about my grandfather. I half expected to discover a shrunken, wrinkled, shell of a man. I knew he was approaching eighty years of age and it was beyond me how a person who drank as he did could live to see so many others die around him.

I knew the area where he lived and began searching Assisted Living and Nursing Homes in the vicinity. I created a list of potential residences using the internet, and was surprised there were so many candidates. I began calling one after another, inquiring of the grandfather I hadn't seen in forty years. Then I remembered how, after many dead-end calls, I had used the internet to find one of the men my father said raped my mother. Though I found many persons of the same name, I was able to single one out, and was confident it was him.

I had found a house owned by my grandfather, but there was no phone listing for the address. I knew the only way to confirm the information was to travel there and see for myself. I booked my flight and once again stepped into the unknown.

The Southern California smog darkened the sun's rays as I pulled off the highway and entered Bryan's neighborhood. The butterflies took flight as I pulled around the corner. *One more left and I'm there,* I thought. Having heard the stories of his drinking and abuse, I knew his Cherokee blood ran deep and it didn't take much alcohol to make it boil.

Slowing the car to a crawl, I approached the house on the corner. I knew my grandfather had family there for years. Not blood relatives, but those of his second wife, Belen. The house was being added onto in the same fashion as many of the homes in the neighborhood. If the houses were not being torn down, they were upgraded or simply left to time. I had studied the maps as if I were going in with a S.W.A.T. team. They were burnt into my psyche so that I knew exactly where I was. His house was just around the corner.

As I straightened out the car, it was there on my left: the house my grandfather had lived in for over three decades—if he was still there. Yellow siding, white awning, and a short veneer of red brick stood behind a narrow strip of grass. It probably looked the same as when he bought it in the early seventies.

In the drive was a '64 Ford pickup with a '69 camper on the back. The truck, rigged for the camper, sported a two-foot-wide back bumper for easy camper access. Next to it was a maroon '72 Sport Coupe. Then, oddly enough, an Olds '88 was parked perpendicular to the others at the bottom of the drive. All these vehicles were somehow squeezed onto a driveway built for two.

My own wheels never stopped turning; I was scared; I was worried someone else would answer the door only to shoo me away. I imagined his second wife's family hiding him away in the dark of the old house; hovering over their inheritance as he nears his eightieth birthday. I was afraid he might be there; the man who had abused my mother and her family for so long. I never touched the brakes.

I parked at the curb after driving around the block to gather my courage. At the very least I wanted to get a picture of his house. I decided I'd steal a snapshot before I was run off, so I retrieved my camera from its bag and went around the block again.

I pulled around the corner once more, this time from the opposite direction; I snapped two shots before coming to a stop: another nondescript photo for the family album. Something to prove, perhaps one day to my own grandson, just how close I got. I killed the engine, returned the camera to the bag, and braced myself for yet another unknown ending.

I had no idea who this man would be, the man whose name I bear. I imagined him short and slumped, as shriveled as his liver must be from years of binge drinking. I didn't know if he'd greet me with open arms or shout me down, pointing me the way to Hell.

As the car door slammed shut behind me, I crossed the street, stepping through the grass because cars blocked the concrete pathways. At the door, I took a deep breath and prodded the tiny doorbell button.

I heard nothing. For at least two minutes I stood there as my stomach sunk farther and farther towards my shoes. *The cars may all be broken down*, I thought. *He's not here.* I knocked on the screen door. The ancient aluminum shook and rattled as my knuckles rapped and tapped. Then, as if from the darkness of my mind, I heard light footsteps approaching the door. The knob shook as the clatter of an old, worn-out lock sprang from the inside.

It seemed to take forever for the wooden door to swing open. I stood there, holding fast to my frail composure, for I knew, one way or another, that I had stirred the winds of change again.

The old man with the worn, leathery face stood much more erect than I expected.

"What can I do for you?" He gently inquired.

"I'm looking for Bryan Mason."

I knew from the old photographs of the young Bryan, that this was indeed him, although I tried not to assume.

"That's me."

I smiled, and allowed myself a brief moment of pride at having unlocked another piece of the past.

"I'm Bryan McGlothin."

He stood there in silence.

"I'm Angie's boy," I added after several seconds' pause.

His mouth opened wide and his white eyes widened and glowed from behind the screen door. As the screen door swung open, I thrust out my hand for a friendly handshake. Knowing the Bryan of the past, I wasn't ready to embrace the man who had wielded such a brutal arm. But he took my hand heartily and drew me into his home.

Stepping into his living room, I closed the door behind me, and the room went black until he flipped the switch. As my eyes adjusted to the new light I felt as though I had just stepped onto a 60s movie set.

There was a Barcalounger at the door with deep cracks in

its faux leather, facing a little TV atop a broken console. Above the TV were three large, tastefully framed pictures. One was of John F. and Robert Kennedy. The middle one was of JFK and his wife Jacqueline. On the right was none other than Lyndon B. Johnson. These framed dignitaries seemed to be looking up and to the right, as if that was the general direction of the future.

As I took in all this nostalgia, Bryan grabbed my arm and directed me to a little photo to the left. On the wall behind his worn recliner was a little boy I recognized all too well. The child stood there, arms to the side, squinting from the sun, with no hint of a grin; it was me at five years old: the same picture my mother had received from my father. I had stood there in this living room, just behind my grandfather, for over 30 years. And all that time, he had greeted me each time he sat in his comfortable chair.

"I thought I'd never see you again," he lamented. "You were my first grandchild, you know."

I nodded agreement. "Yeah, Guess you're right."

"When I got up this morning, I never thought I'd be getting a surprise like this today." He smiled and the Cherokee lines dug deeper across his cheeks.

We sat there for a moment and made small talk before he asked if I'd eaten breakfast. Of course I had, but I knew where he was going with this and wanted to follow. So I lied.

"No, I haven't."

"Well, you want to have breakfast?"

"Absolutely."

"Good. Let me get my face cleaned up and we'll go." He rose from the chair and began to make his way across the room, before taking a detour to explain a few photos on the wall.

He finally made it to the restroom and I looked carefully around the room as I waited. It was surprisingly clean. There was no mothball odor seeping from the closets; no tobacco emanating from the curtains. The table next to the chair was covered in opened mail, old newspapers, a clean ashtray, and several mini Snickers. On the coffee table, dust-covered frames harbored black and white portraits. These were so closely packed in the middle that they seemed to be propping each other up, leaving only room enough for dust to accumulate on the remaining surface. No-one in this crowded collection seemed familiar to me.

A photo of a young Bryan, in his WWII Air Force uniform, hung neatly beside his father's military picture. Wilton, my great-grandfather, had enlisted just after World War I. Next to Wilton was his wife, my grandfather's mother. She posed there, shyly, at about age eighteen: a beautiful young woman she was with her dark Indian complexion. His father, placed in the most honorable-looking frame, was a younger great-grandfather than the man I had seen in the stack of photos at my mother's home.

Once more, I was reminded of the family I should have known and loved; people of whom I should have colorful memories, preserved in black and white.

Although I didn't recognize everyone, there were several familiar faces. My cousin Sherry, whom I met for the first time in spring 2004, was just two frames away from my little snapshot. With her big smile, the teenager watched over me for decades before I knew her. My grandmother, Lola Mae, was absent, as were others from my family. My grandfather had moved on and married Belen in the 60s, not long after Lola Mae's death. I suppose there was no reason why he shouldn't begin a new life after losing his first wife, but why would he leave behind others he should have loved?

Belen had died over ten years ago. I wondered if he had spent that time here in his recliner, alone, in this darkness. He had pointed out the pictures of Belen's children, some in wedding white, but where were they? Did they offer him the same time and effort as when their mother was alive? Or did he run them off with his drinking and badgering?

He returned from the back room, hair slicked and looking refreshed. We jumped in his huge Olds '88, hit the road, and cruised over to one of his usual diners to share a breakfast— our first in forty years.

As the host asked, "How many?" Bryan rang out, "two!"

It sounded if he'd just found a new girlfriend.

We sat across from one another and discussed family, the past, and the future. As I listened to his stories, I stared as deeply as I could into his dark eyes. The tales of his alcohol abuse and violence, of his disappearances, flashed through my mind. I wanted to see this man I had heard so much about, to be unafraid. I wanted to see him, and to know him, so I would know where to stand; find my own footing. But no matter how hard I tried, all I could see was a gentle old man: a grandfather, excited as a crisp Christmas morning to see his lost grandson.

His eyes were coal-black, but I could see no demons. His face was filled with deep lines, but not from anger. He was sober and caring. He laughed aloud at his own tales of traveling the country with Belen. He was simply my grandfather.

When I mentioned my mother, his joyful smile gave way to a shamefaced frown. He admitted that the last time he saw her was just before she and Jack left for Oklahoma, in the early eighties.

I told him about all the family I had found over the last

year. His expression revealed that he knew everyone had a story to tell about him, but he didn't approach the issue and neither did I.

He soon asked if my father was still in "that religion." I confirmed this and then told him how, after years of confinement in the Watchtower, I was able to escape.

"That's good. That religion was the reason for most of our fights... between Lola and me," he responded.

He told me how she continually tried to convert him, and how he told her she could do whatever she wanted but he wasn't becoming a Jehovah's Witness.

He recalled how, when my mother was a little girl, he asked what everyone wanted for Christmas. Lola, my grandmother, retorted with "We don't celebrate Christmas." Bryan told her that, under his roof, they do celebrate Christmas, and he was buying presents.

"Think of them as just gifts if you want, but I'm buying Christmas presents for everyone," he told her.

We discussed all the family we could conjure up and how so many are dying off.

"I'm gonna be left here all alone," he said.

Soon enough the waitress came around with the check as we both grabbed at it. She smiled broadly as she heard Bryan say, "I'll get it. It's not every day I get to buy my grandson breakfast."

"That's so sweet," she said, walking away.

I didn't resist. I let the proud grandfather treat his grandson and we went on our way, no-one the wiser.

As we left the restaurant in his "boat" he asked, "You in a hurry to get anywhere?"

"No," I replied.

"Well, I'm going to see Belen. Would you like to go?" He

asked.

I knew where she was, and I was happy to accept his invitation.

As we drove through town towards the cemetery, he pointed out the places he frequented: the automotive shop where he used to hang out with the "guys" until the owner sold it, the car wash he referred to as "his."

He told harrowing stories of WWII duty, as a radio operator in the Air Force, and recalled how they often lost pilots to the flack exploding all around them. He reminisced about flying exuberantly around the Eiffel Tower as he returned liberated French to their own country.

He drove like a young man. His mind is sharp and he gets around well. We rounded curves on what seemed like two wheels and used the full four barrels over the 3.8 more times than I can count. Along the way we had good conversation as well as moments of awkward silence. We arrived at the well-manicured, but brown, lawns and pulled right up to Belen's spot.

The grass over her was groomed with more care than that of the surrounding lawn. Three concrete vases imbedded in the earth were filled with vibrant flowers in plenty of water.

He popped the trunk and retrieved a red rag, approached her marble headstone, and got down on all fours. Then he began cleaning and polishing it as though it were a new car. Over and over he crossed the marble with the cloth until the shine was perfect.

"You come here a lot?"

"Every day," he said. "Thirty-eight dollars and forty-two cents every week, in fresh flowers."

"Every week," he repeated, after a pause. As a retired single man, he explained, he had plenty of time to visit her. I began to feel that, perhaps, he was very alone in his little world.

He talked of the great times he had with Belen over the twenty-eight years they were together.

He related how he used to do his own yard work and he'd come inside on hot summer days and ask Belen for change to buy a couple of beers. She'd go off, and give him a hard time.

"But she always gave in," He added.

He checked the water in the vases, and finding them full, returned the cloth to the trunk and said goodbye to Belen. We turned and left her to rest.

As we left, we discussed the places in the area where family had lived; he asked if I still had more time.

"Sure," I replied.

"Then I'll take you to where your mother used to live." Now this was exciting—and a welcome surprise. I had a list of addresses that I intended to visit, gleaned from old letters. I was happy to get an early start.

Off we went again, straightening the corners, flying down the highway, until we came to the airport. After winding through a residential neighborhood, we arrived at a school. He slowed the car to a crawl and lamented, "Oh no, looks like they tore it down."

With a sigh, I realized how the addresses I had, the life my mother lived, were decades in the past. I feared they would all be replaced with strip malls.

The car crawled past the school as Bryan perked up.

"There it is!" He said as we topped the hill.

At the bottom, behind two towering pine trees, stood the house my mother and Jack rented for close to fourteen years. This was the house from where my mother wrote several letters to my father. In fact it was in this house where she wrote him just one year before attempting suicide, pleading to see me, or at the very least, for permission to send me a picture of herself. My mother spent years there crying over her desperate letters, wondering where I was. She'd traveled from that house to Oklahoma to find me more than once. The house looked as lonely as I imagine her to have been.

I sat in the car and imagined her sitting there on the stoop, heartbroken, until she saw me running up the road to see her once again. In my mind, her face was filled with tearful joy as she ran to meet me.

We finally made our way back to his house and I sat on the sofa like a little boy hanging on his grandpa's every word.

"You know how I got that picture?" He asked, pointing to my little photo on the wall.

"I thought you probably got it from my mom. She's got the same one." I had assumed my father sent more than one copy to my mother and she gave one to her father, but this was not the case.

The little snapshot of me was passed on to him by the people who managed the "Hidden Valley Trailer Park" on E. Garvey in Baldwin Park. This was the trailer park where Lola Mae complained of the noise and smog from the highway, and where Bryan lived for years after her death. Irwin and Helen Kramer, also Jehovah's Witnesses, managed the trailer park for years. When my father sent the picture to my mother around 1971, he also sent a copy to the Kramers. The day I was born, my father called the office at the trailer park and spoke to them. They grabbed my grandfather and brought him to their office so he could take the call and hear personally of the new arrival. "Hello grandpa!" were my father's words to Bryan.

The first time my father took me by stealth, telling my

mother he was on vacation and wanted to buy clothes for me, it was from that very place.

My father, no doubt, knew they were Witnesses. He and my mother had visited there many times during her pregnancy, after her family left McLoud and settled there. Lola, also being a Witness, would have informed my parents of this. The Kramers also organized my grandmother's funeral. My father may have felt sure they knew he had taken me, and wanted to let his fellow Witnesses know I was physically fine.

"You're his grandfather, you should have the picture," Irwin had said as he gave my grandfather the little picture of me, his first grandchild.

These could well be the same people my father spoke of when I was eighteen, after I told him I wanted to invite my mother to my wedding. He said he contacted old friends of her family who owned a property with cabins. Though my mother's family had moved to a trailer park, they actually live in little apartments on the property. My family referred to them as "cabins." Dad had told me they said my mother overdosed on drugs and was committed to a mental institution, where she died.

The Kramers did not live in the "Hidden Valley Trailer Park" in 1982. They moved out before my grandfather left in 1971–72. My mother attempted suicide in 1973, at which time Bryan Mason says he had no contact with the Kramers. So did the Kramers and my father keep contact with each other through the years?

Perhaps they had heard about my mother's attempted suicide and told my father. Regardless, I know there is no way my father would have invited her to my wedding. He had told too many lies and committed too many horrible deeds. To put me in contact with her would have revealed his nasty secrets.

Could they have told him about her near-lethal cocktail, and that she was not the same person afterward? Perhaps my father heard the whole story and, knowing my mother was still alive, told me she had died? Or perhaps he just made the whole story up and it was all coincidence.

He told me, when I was a boy, that my mother "liked to party." It was therefore a perfect story to say my mother had overdosed, obviously at one of her "parties," and died in an insane asylum, of all places.

This is exactly what I thought. That my mother turned her back on Jehovah God and all that is pure as she embraced Satan firmly in her wretched bosom, all the way to her ungodly and debauched demise. As a young Witness this subdued my yearning. The only thing I know for certain is that, when my father said my mother was dead, she manifestly was not.

I sat taking in the flood of new information, scribbling notes as fast as I could. Bryan continued, telling me how Belen straightened him out, convincing him to control his drinking, at least until 1991 when she passed away. Then, with the help of concerned friends and family, he was able to obtain enough Vodka to drink himself into a coma. A week later he woke up, and has never taken a drink since. Now there are no empty beer cans or whiskey flasks on his table, but instead many vitamin and herb bottles.

Though my grandfather says WWII had no adverse effect on him, other family members feel otherwise. He is quoted as saying, "You can say you don't believe in God, but when shrapnel is coming up into your plane, anyone can believe in God."

Today, I see the gentleness of my grandfather, though I cannot forget his tempestuous past. I am very happy he has found peace with his sobriety, but still saddened by the drunken abuse he heaped upon his wife and children as a young man. But people change all the time; I feel Bryan deserves another chance, and I am happy to have him back in my life. I know my mother misses him and loves him very much. If she is willing to forgive, then who am I to stand against him?

Traveling so many emotional miles, meeting my lost grandfather, and finally coming to another discovery, was deeply rewarding.

The next Christmas, I called him from my mother's house. And after more than fifteen years, she spoke to her father.

June 23, 72

Fred,
  I received your most welcomed letter. Thank you very much for the papers that Bryan did. They are really good. He prints really nice. Also, thank you very-very much for the pictures. He is the cutiest little guy I've ever seen. I love him so very much. I hope that someday you'll find it in your heart to let me see him. Does he know that I'm his mother? Have you told him about me?
  Is he going to be tall? I imagine he's pretty tall now. What grade is he in?
  Fred, I'm sorry that you

The first page of Angie's letter to Fred,
pleading for news of Bryan.

2.

lost your grand-
mother. What will
happen to your
uncle now?

My grandmother
Mason died March
15th, 72 and Mam-
maw Turner died
the 21st of April, 72.

If you have told
Bryan about me, and
you don't care, could I
send him a picture of
me? I hope that he doesn't
have a bad problem with
his teeth. Do you think
his teeth will be straight?
If he needs braces - I could
help you get them.

Fred, it was such a
long time between letters,
could you write more often?
Please? Please let me
know how Bryan is doing

The second page of Angie's letter to Fred,
pleading to see Bryan, and for news of him.

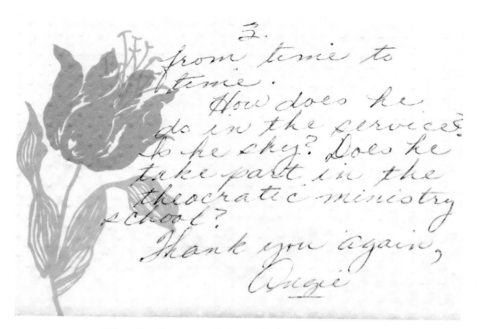

3.

from time to time.

How does he do in the services? Is he shy? Does he take part in the theocratic ministry school?

Thank you again,

Angie

The final page of Angie's letter to Fred, pleading for news of her son.

The beige building on the right is the convenience store where Fred abducted Bryan. This photograph was taken from Lillie and William Stamper's yard.

Dear Lucille and all,

I recieved a letter from Freddie and baby. They are doing fine, altho they have been sick.

Freddie sent me a picture of Bryan and his is so cute. And he sure has grown.

I've written Freddie another letter. Would you mail it as soon as you can?

Take care and tell everyone hello for me.

As ever,
Angie

Angie's letter to Fred McGlothin's parents, Buck and Lucille (left) asking them to forward her pleading letter to him.

Bryan's first glimpse of his mother: Fred
McGlothin and Angie Mason on their
wedding day.

Angie at the grave of her
mother, Lola Mae Mason,
in 1964.

Bryan Lee McGlothin, aged 13
months, in 1965. This photo
was sent to Angie Turner, his
great-grandmother.

The photographs on this and the facing page were sent to Angie by Fred McGlothin while he was hiding Bryan by moving repeatedly.

This photograph also appears on the dust jacket. It was taken in a park in Lewsiville, just after the abduction.

Bryan, aged 5, in Paradise Valley, AZ. Bryan D. Mason displayed this photograph on the wall near his lounger.

Bryan, aged 6, in Arkansas.

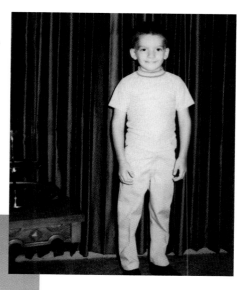

Bryan, aged 7, in Arkansas.

Bryan, after his father
and stepmother
moved to Texas.

Bryan (age uncertain) taken by his mother
shortly before he was abducted.

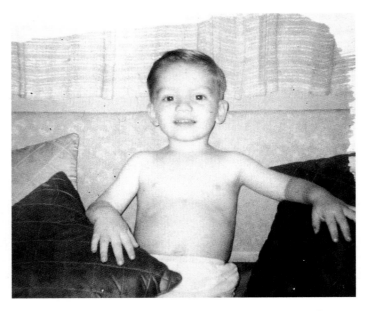

Bryan aged 2 years and 2 months, taken by
his mother shortly before he was abducted.

Stella and Benjamin Ephraim Poindexter

Nora and Wilton Mason with Sherry and Angie

Bryan and Lola Mae Mason (their daughters are below).

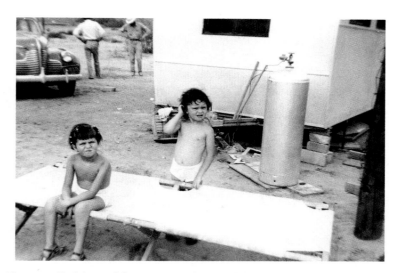

Sherry (left) and her sister Angie Mason, Bryan's mother.
Bryan Mason and George W. Turner are in the background.

Angie and George W. Turner on their wedding day.

Angie and G. W. Turner

This photograph of Bryan McGlothin's mother,
Angie Stamper, was used to create the artwork on
the outer dust jacket of the book. It was taken
in 1970, when she was 23.

Angie with Bryan.

Bryan with his daughter Anna the last time he
saw her, in 2004.

Angie and Bryan on the first day they saw each other after more than thirty years. The roses in the background on the right are the first flowers Angie ever received from her son.

Lillie, Jack, and Angie Stamper in 1997, during Bryan's
reunion visit: the first smiles of many.

Bryan D. Mason enjoying breakfast with his grandson,
Bryan McGlothin, whom he has not seen in forty years.

Jack and Angie Stamper on their wedding day in Las Vegas, March 1970.

Bryan and Evelyne.

Chapter 12

He's about the best baby I've ever seen

It was the early sixties; Bryan and Lola Mae had already parted, divorced, reconciled, and reinstated their marriage. Bryan says it was obvious Lola's illness was taking its toll. Some say he suggested they get back together because it was clear the kids would need him. Others say they remarried because they couldn't bear to be apart, even if they fought like pit bulls when they were together.

Lola had been stricken with rheumatic fever as a child. This, along with her cigarette smoking, led to her adult illness.

While living in Merana, Bryan had worked as a machinist at Hughes Aircraft, but jobs in Oklahoma were scarce. He settled for work as an attendant at the Champion gas station, earning a meager wage compared to his income for machining aircraft parts: "fifty-five dollars a week for seven days' work."

My parents met early in 1963 at a Jehovah's Witness Assembly in the Oklahoma City area. Lola Mae's mother, Angie Leslie, was the holiest of holy rollers. She was a devout Pentecostal, not a Witness, as was her mother, Stella Frances Wall. Stella's husband, Benjamin Ephraim Poindexter, would have nothing to do with the fevered group, but the Poindexters were accustomed to attending tent revivals, singing into the late night, feeding off the impassioned cadence of the preacher, and witnessing the healing of the lame and afflicted; I'm sure.

Angie Turner later turned to the Jehovah's Witnesses to feed her hunger for religious guidance and expression. Her husband, George, attended the meetings with his wife, but he was never baptized.

In the past the Jehovah's Witnesses prophesied that the end of the world as we know it would come in 1914. They later proclaimed, at the time Angie Turner became involved, that Christ actually began ruling in heaven in 1914, and The End would come before the generation of 1914 died off. The Witnesses were—and are—a cultish doomsday organization, which filled the emotional and spiritual needs of my great-grandmother; she shared this passion with her daughters. This same affinity for doomsday religion is also a general trait of my father's family.

My father asked for my mother's hand in marriage almost immediately after their first meeting. But my grandfather was opposed to his youngest daughter marrying at the tender age of sixteen.

Lola would beg her husband, literally on her knees, to allow their daughter to marry the handsome servant from McLoud. In the sixties, the law required the signature of both parents for such a young person to be wed, and Bryan wanted no part of it. At times, Lola and my mother would show up at his work asking him to sign the paper. Once, my father drove to his future father-in-law's place of employment to ask for Angie's hand in marriage once more. Bryan was upset and afraid he'd lose his job. Feeling as though the whole world was against him, he gave in and signed the paper.

Fred, twenty-five, and Angie, sixteen, married quickly on June 5, 1963, in the Kingdom Hall of Jehovah's Witnesses in

Ada. The reception was held at the Mason home, between the Oklahoma cities of Ada and Stonewall. In preparation, Bryan purchased two half-gallon jugs of whiskey for the festivities. As luck would have it, none of the Witnesses touched Bryan's offering, so he had it all to himself.

He was so intoxicated, in fact, that he didn't show up at work for days. The owner of the gas station was forced to hire someone else to do his job. As a consequence, Bryan and Lola Mason decided to move to McLoud, near my mother and their new son-in-law. Bryan found work there with my father's cousins, roofing and hauling hay. This grueling work did not agree with my grandfather.

This was at the time when my father worked for Shine Rhodes, repairing TVs in McLoud, and my mother was a housewife. Everything seemed fine in their marriage for some time, but within months my grandfather grew weary of struggling with the dead-end jobs of central Oklahoma, and announced he was returning to California were work was plentiful.

Bryan suggested his wife, Lola Mae, stay in Ada with her family because of her worsening health. But Lola wanted to be with her husband and she accompanied him to California. Sherry soon followed. The next September, my mother and father attended the eight-day International Convention of Jehovah's Witnesses at the Rose Bowl in Pasadena, California. My mother, suffering from morning sickness, only attended the first day or two of the assembly. It was a long drive from McLoud to the Los Angeles area, and my mother's family was still living with Lola's brother and his wife, Dub and Shug. The house was already full with the two families. My parents, therefore, had to find alternative accommodation. Some family friends living in Baldwin Park had a room available after their son left home to live with a friend. The couple offered their son's vacant room to the expectant mother and her new husband. Pasadena was a short drive from Baldwin Park, and after all, they were good friends with my mother. They were William and Lillie Stamper. If the name sounds familiar, it is because *Jack Stamper* is their son; he married my mother in 1970. This is the same Stamper my father couldn't quite remember, "guessing" it was something like Stamper, Stemper, or perhaps Stomper.

My father knew the Stampers well. My mother called Lillie "Mom."

My mother and her family moved just three houses down from the Stampers when she was nine. The two families quickly made friends. Jack tells me how, during their early teens, my mother and Sherry regarded his home as a haven from their father's abuse.

It was Jack's mother, Lillie, who begged my mother not to take me with them to the cemetery on the day that I was abducted.

"I wouldn't know him walkin' down the street today, but I've met him two or three times," Jack told me.

My father's uncle, Jeb, said that during this time, my father would "spend too much time with the boys," leaving my mother alone at home. Jeb spoke to my father about neglecting his responsibilities as a husband, but his counsel fell on deaf ears.

It was also in their first few months of marriage that my mother confided in Lola Mae and other trusted family members that, if he became angry with her, my father would grab her breasts and twist her nipples until they were bruised. My sixteen-year-old mother made several calls to her mother, begging for guidance. Lola Mae reminded my mother that she was married to a servant of the Jehovah's Witnesses. The marriage may not have been perfect, Lola reasoned, but there was nothing better than a spiritually strong man for a husband. Considering the abuse Lola Mae suffered at the hands of her own husband—and the countless times she returned to the violence—she may not have been the best marriage counselor regarding spousal abuse.

My mother's early life—her formative years—was powerfully influenced by her father's physical abuse of all the women in his household. The poisonous legacy of domestic violence is its spreading, growing consequences. In my mother's case, she was unusually vulnerable and at a high risk from domestic violence as an adult because of the environment in which she learned, as a little girl, how to be a wife, a sister, and a mother; not to mention how a husband and father are supposed to run a household.

Immediately upon marriage, at sixteen and with no more than a tenth-grade education, she went where her childhood directed her: under the control of another older man, with her mother's encouragement and support. My father was a comparatively seasoned twenty-five, with a high school diploma, a blossoming position in the church, and a stable job in a desirable trade. It was understandable for her to be intimidated in such an unbalanced situation; even after she had lost contact with me, it's said she remained intimidated as she had been in her youth.

Not only was my mother confused in her new marriage and feeling lonely in McLoud, but her mother's failing health was weighing on her. She knew her mother's health was worsening in the basin of Southern California where the smog was a way of life. No sooner did they return from the Witnesses' convention in Pasadena than my mother heard from her sister, who wrote of Lola's near-fatal asthma attack. My mother must have felt the need to go to her mother's side and care for her. But, married and pregnant, she must also have known she had no other option than to keep in touch by letter.

Two months after returning from the Jehovah's Witnesses' Convention, on November 15th 1963, George W. Turner, my mother's grandfather, died. This was not unexpected, because he had been diagnosed with cancer six months prior, by which time his body was consumed with the deadly cells.

My mother had spent many years living near her grandparents and this significant loss must have compounded her emotional difficulties. George's death did, however, result in a visit with her mother and Sherry. My grandfather gave Lola Mae and Sherry the bus fare to attend the funeral. It must have been a bittersweet reunion: my mother was elated to see her kin, but Lola Mae was so ill, she barely weighed a hundred pounds.

My mother was desperate to have her mother with her in Ada for the birth of her first child, but several obstacles stood in the way. The first, though not the hardest, was my grandfather, as my grandmother indicates in a letter to my mother, dated January 13th 1964:

> *I don't know if we will get to come back or not Angie. That sure is a long way. Your dad said if I went & left him any more that he was really going to have a ball while I was gone.*

Since my grandfather and other women had been mentioned more than once in the same sentence, I'm sure my mother knew what Lola Mae was insinuating.

Again, in March 1964, Lola Mae answers her daughter's

plea to be with her:

> *Angie with all the trouble I'm having with your daddy & all, I don't think I'd better come back there. Besides you would have to send me the money. Your daddy said he wouldn't give it to me.*

Such was life for Lola Mae; although Bryan made it impossible for his wife to support their daughter at a time when she needed her mother deeply, Lola's state of health also kept her from my mother's side. Her asthma was taking an increasingly heavy toll.

In a letter mailed November 12th 1963, Lola tried to educate my mother from a distance, by reminding her of things taught before she married:

> *Angie, before you ever married, I taught you about those old wives tales. So from now on if you don't understand something, ask your doctor or do research in the Awake bound volumes.*

Although well-intentioned, this suggestion must have aggravated my mother's isolation, since it relegated the special relationship between a loving mother and her pregnant daughter to a lonely reading assignment.

My mother later developed problems in her pregnancy. On January 21st 1964, Lola Mae writes:

> *It might be pretty tough on you laying around, but it might be the best thing for you to do. If you lose all your water you might have a dry birth & that is not good.*

151

The problem resolved enough that my mother was able to carry me to term and I was born in Ada on a Monday evening, May 4th 1964. We left the hospital the following Thursday. The doctor advised her to stay with friends in Ada until Sunday, as McLoud is some distance from Ada and she would be closer to the hospital if she or her new baby needed medical attention.

My mother wrote a letter to Lola, on May 11th. It is one of two letters I have from her in which she refers to me. She begins by expressing hope that Lola Mae is in better health and gaining weight. Then she turns her attention to me:

> *Well it's four o'clock and Bryan Lee is asleep. He's about the best baby I've ever seen. The only time he ever cries is when he's hungry or wet. Last night he wouldn't go back to sleep so I got him in bed with us & was nursing him. I went to sleep 3:30 am and when I woke up again 6:30 am he was getting himself some more dinner. (ha)*

It was endearing and moving to read these loving words from such a young girl upon the birth of her first child; it was all the more touching because I am that child. She later says:

> *Be back in a minute. Bryan Lee's awake and he's hungry. Well, I'm back & I'm holding Bryan & he's getting his dinner. He sure smacks and gulps. He's a week old today.*

Later in this letter, she expresses her excited anticipation of a planned family trip to Southern California: her first opportunity to show off the new arrival to her family.

The day after she mailed this letter, on May 12th, at just thirty-eight years old, Lola Mae died of "cardio-respiratory failure." She passed without reading her daughter's loving, joyful words—and without ever seeing her grandchild.

Upon hearing of this sad event, my mother's uncle Dub called his sister Vera, who lived near Ada. Vera and her second husband, Bitty, decided in their grief to make the sixty-mile drive to McLoud and tell my mother personally. As they made hasty preparations to leave, we came down the drive as if by divine intervention. I was only eight days old. Vera gave my mother the bad news as gently as she could. My mother began to scream hysterically and collapsed to the ground, almost dropping me. My father, trying to take control of the situation, slapped my mother's face in an effort to restore her sanity. She knew Lola Mae was desperately ill, but the seventeen-year-old never thought her mother would leave her like that. It was bad enough they were so far apart, but for her mother to be gone so suddenly—and at such a time—was too much.

Several of my mother's family in the Ada area traveled to my grandmother's funeral. There was ample room in the station wagon for my mother and me to accompany them. When I was a child, my father told me that my mother couldn't make the fourteen-hundred mile trip because she had a difficult delivery. I understand now that the reason my mother and I didn't attend Lola Mae's funeral is because my father forbade her to go.

"He used you as an excuse," my grandfather said.

My mother, at seventeen, had lost her grandfather, given birth to a baby, and then lost her mother who was over a thousand miles away. She must have felt a deep sense of loss and longing to be with her family.

We made the trip to California two months later, in July, as previously planned. Instead of going there to show off her newborn son, the purpose of the trip was now to say goodbye to my grandmother in person, by visiting her gave.

It is likely that we also visited the Stampers, so mom could show off her new son to her "number two mom," Lillie.

Between the death of her mother and our trip to California, Aunt Sherry married a man named Eddie Franco. After visiting my grandmother's grave and family, my mother and father, along with Sherry and Eddie, took a quick trip to Tijuana, Mexico. As a young child I'd always heard my father joking about Tijuana, and how loose the atmosphere was there. We made several trips to the border towns in my youth. Judy, my mother's cousin, at home with her own newborn, was kind enough to keep me while the surviving sisters spent time together along with their husbands.

Ultimately, when faced with saying goodbye to her surviving family and returning to Oklahoma, my mother froze and refused to leave. My father had to talk to her for some time before she would turn her back on the setting sun. I believe despair may have led to an emotional breakdown for my mother. She knew she had a home and family back in McLoud, but with the loss of her mother, she was reluctant to leave her family and all that was familiar. It was an omen of the rough road ahead.

They returned home and my father continued to work, while my mother became progressively more unhappy and restless. Soon, she would leave McLoud with me—but not as a thief in the night, as my father presented it many years ago.

Only about a month after returning to McLoud, in mid-August 1964, my mother called her sister and Eddie, begging them to drive from California and pick up the two of us. She sounded desperate. They invited my grandfather and left after Eddie finished work on Friday. They drove straight through and arrived in Oklahoma the next day.

This was the first time my mother left McLoud alone with me. My father described how he came home from work to find that we had left without warning. I had only this perspective until spring 2004, when I spoke to my Aunt Sherry and her ex-husband Eddie, then confirmed their story with my grandfather, I know the truth of that fateful day. It was the day my father began to grow his own conspiracy.

My mother and father's marital problems were worsening. I'm sure she was in deep mourning for her mother and her grandfather George, who had departed within a few months of each other. Traveling to visit surviving family in California had only sharpened her already-keen need.

Eddie recalls the trip with my grandfather well, because Bryan was very upset about not being able to get a drink in Arizona on a Sunday.

They arrived in McLoud near midnight. My mother did not know her way around town, so she told her sister to drive to Shine Rhode's home to get directions to her house. Shine was my father's employer and my grandfather knew him and where he lived. This may have made my father even more indignant. McLoud was, and still is, a very small town; no doubt the story of my mother rapidly made its way round the community network, passing from neighbor to neighbor in the course of everyday life in the hair salon, the barber shop, the grocery store, the diner...

When Bryan and Eddie arrived at Shine's home, Bryan beat on the door until he roused him from bed. Shine opened the door and squinted out into the night with sleepy eyes. "Bryan, is that you?" He asked.

"Yeah, it's me, Shine."

"You sure picked a hell of a time to visit," he grumbled.

My grandfather obtained the directions and they were back on the road. As they neared our house, the crickets appeared in Biblical numbers. The chirping was deafening and the crunching under the tires was sharp.

"They were so thick on the road my '55 Pontiac was sliding all over the place," my uncle remembered.

As soon as they arrived, they began packing our things into Eddie's car. It was less than an hour before they were on the road again.

"Freddie and Angie seemed to have argued all they could by the time we arrived," Bryan said.

My mother had told my father she needed time to think, and was going to stay with her father for a while to figure things out. My father said goodbye and we left; she didn't sneak out. There was no chicanery, no vanishing act while my father was working. For decades I believed my mother started the tug-o'-war and my father did what any loving father would do by searching for his abducted son. Now that time has caught up to those who squandered it, the truth speaks freely.

My mother and I stayed with my grandfather when we arrived in California. Bryan clearly recalls her fragile state of mind.

"Your mother was very confused at the time and I don't think she had any intention of returning with you."

But less than a month later my father appeared, unannounced, on Bryan's front porch. He said he had come up on vacation to spend time with us. Mom was surprised, but it is clear he knew exactly where we were: right where she told him.

"She seemed happy he came out," Eddie said. "Seemed

she was excited that Freddie wanted her back."

Perhaps because my father made such a long and unexpected journey, my mother began to believe he really cared about her and truly wanted to support her through her emotional crisis.

He told her he had family or friends in the area and wanted to visit them with me. When she asked to go as well, my father suggested she stay behind, saying that, since he had not seen me in close to a month, he and I could spend some quality time together. He also told her he wanted to shop for clothes for me.

My mother was not running from my father or hiding me from anyone. As far as she was concerned they were still a married couple, even if they having problems. Confident my father was being truthful, she handed me over.

My grandfather described a sense of foreboding, saying, "I told her not to let him take you. He drove up in a taxi. I knew something wasn't right, but I had to get to work. They were a married couple anyway."

As the hours went by, my mother became fretful. She waited—and she waited. The day turned to night and my father and I did not return.

"I don't know what he did with you. All you had on was a diaper. No shoes even," Bryan said.

He never took me shopping. He had no relatives in Southern California. He directed the taxi straight to the airport and flew back to Oklahoma with me in his arms.

When I was fifteen, he called my mother a "liar" and a "conniver." He convinced me, from when I was only eight, that she was the instigator in the child-swapping that took place for two years, building the impression that he was compelled to react to my mother's attempts to destroy our family.

In truth, it was he who first plotted to seize me.

Had my father been more patient with his adolescent wife, more sensitive to her emotional distress, things might have turned out differently. My mother's choice to go to California may not have been the best decision for the family. But she was as naïve and inexperienced as any other teenager, isolated in the small town of McLoud with her remote and unsupportive older husband.

Frantic, my mother immediately returned to McLoud to find me. She left California behind to reunite with her child and husband, but it may have been the worst decision of her life.

Chapter 13

He was supposed to set an example

Immediately upon bringing me back to McLoud, my father filed a court petition on September 15th 1964, for "separate maintenance, custody of said minor child, and restraining order" (a legal separation) in Pottawatomie County. The petition stated:

> ... *since the birth of said child, defendant has been guilty of gross neglect of duty and extreme cruelty toward plaintiff and toward said minor child, including acts of brutality committed on said minor child, and that, therefore, she is an unfit person to have custody of said minor child and is [unable] to give the same good home with proper surroundings...*

Quite an amazing charge: "acts of brutality." What about our trip to California the previous July, and then to Mexico? If she was committing acts of brutality against me, why didn't my father save me then, instead of taking us on vacation? Why did he allow her to take me to California in the first place, if she was abusive?

I questioned my father's brother, Ray, and his wife Ruth, about my mother treating me poorly. Ruth told of a time when I had blood in my urine. My father's mother, Lucille, told my mother I needed more water. As the story goes, my mother didn't like being told what to do by her mother-in-law, so she refused to give me extra water. I was then taken to the doctor, who said I was dehydrated. Ruth says the doctor was very upset my mother didn't heed the advice. Though he may have scolded the new mother, he did not report any bruising or obvious physical abuse. Neither Ray nor Ruth ever heard my father speak of my mother abusing me. My mother's sister Sherry, her ex-husband Eddie, and her cousin Judy, have all confirmed in the past few years that they had never seen my mother treat me harshly.

My father told me she once threw me across the room onto a bed. But if she had been abusive to such a degree, I would have been hospitalized at some point. I believe my father would have confided in his family about the abuse, or reported the cruelty to the authorities. He never did, perhaps because it never happened.

He may have felt—or been advised—that the only chance at custody of his son and the surest way to remove his wife from the picture was to say (whether truthfully or not) that she was abusive and a threat to my welfare or life. In the sixties, it was very rare for a husband to win custody of the children unless the mother was on drugs, a florid alcoholic, or *a physical threat to the child*.

Could my father have lied in court? He was a servant in the Jehovah's Witness Organization. He was supposed to set an example for the rest of the flock. As a Witness, and espe-cially as a servant, he was supposed to stand above those who are of the *world*. The court's dominion, to a Witness, is *worldly* and as such, of inferior status to the Watchtower. At that time my mother was also a Witness; therefore his priority may have been to protect his standing in the society rather than concern himself with a worldly judge.

On September 18th 1964, my father's lawyer, John L. Green, published a notice of the separation suit in the *County Democrat*, a newspaper once published in Shawnee, Oklahoma.

My father claimed, erroneously, that my mother was not a resident of Oklahoma. The lawyer also sent a letter to what my father said was her last-known address, informing her she was being sued for a separation, but I'm sure she never received it. She had already followed us back to Oklahoma, and soon found a temporary restraining order in place: a result of my father's lawsuit. Court records show that the suit was never prosecuted, probably because he simply did not pursue the case.

By October, he had taken her back. My father, though, may have had a diabolical reason for "reconciliation."

On December 31st 1964, when I was eight months old, my father filed for divorce in Lincoln County Oklahoma. The divorce papers show that my father toned down the accusations he previously made in the separation suit, alleging that "...the defendant has been guilty of extreme cruelty and gross neglect of duty." An order to serve my mother was issued on January 12th 1965, but she was not easy to locate. My father first said she was living with a man named James Berry. The sheriff was directed to go "3¾ miles North of McLoud, Oklahoma, second house, brick siding, on left side." She would not be found there.

New instructions stated that "Angie Lenora McGlothin is now staying at the home of Mrs. Custer in McLoud. The house is located three blocks west of the Prince Grocery and then turn south to the third house on the east side of the street." This was another dead-end.

A new summons was issued to find her at the "Custer Rooming board." New directions were given to the authorities: "Old Conoco station that is closed down at 270 & 3 one block east & one block north on east side." Then a handwritten note: "Subject works at 62 Café in Harrah and lives with lady who operates same." The summons was again returned unfulfilled to the judge. My mother remained elusive.

I believe she did work at the 62 Café for a short time. In a letter from her sister, dated February 14th, just one month after the first summons, Sherry says:

> Boy, you never run out of trouble do you. I thought maybe they were trying to help you out—the people you were working for I mean. You better hurry up and get another job...

The letter was addressed to "Mrs. Sam Hopson." My mother was not staying there when the letter arrived, so it was forwarded to her attorney, J. Hugh Herndon, in Midwest City. My aunt continues her letter by speculating about my father's whereabouts:

> Do you think Fred will ever be caught up with? I think he's in McLoud and if you stay long enough he'll have to come out. I don't believe his lawyer got a letter from Kentucky.

This letter was in reply to an earlier one from my mother. My father had to have been missing for several weeks, after filing for divorce. Aunt Sherry's prediction was wide of the mark: he had taken me to Kentucky. Once again, without my mother's knowledge, he had fled with me under his arm, before I was even a year old. This is why my mother kept moving from place to place; she was searching for me. She probably did not receive her sister's letter for some time. She had tried to become invisible, hoping to catch up with my father in the McLoud area. But Sherry was right about one thing; my father filed for divorce, apparently to throw her off the scent while he took the opportunity to get to Kentucky.

During the three-month period between the first suit, for legal separation, on September 15th, and the second, for divorce, on December 31st, the unthinkable happened.

There are only two circumstances under which a married member of the Jehovah's Witness Organization may remarry, the first being widowhood. The *only* other reason is if the other mate commits adultery and they are divorced. That's it. If, after divorcing your mate *for reasons other than adultery,* you cannot obtain a scriptural divorce from the Watchtower, you cannot remarry; the new marriage would be invalid because you are still *scripturally* wedded to your previous spouse. In this situation, a Witness will be judged adulterous and disfellowshipped from the congregation. This is where the darkest part of the story comes into play.

My parents' fleeting reunion marks the time period during which my mother was raped, for which the Watchtower Organization disfellowshipped her for adultery. This, in turn, furthered my father's twin objectives of an open-and-shut "worldly" legal dissolution and the coveted scriptural divorce from his Watchtower brethren, allowing him the opportunity to remarry: to have a clean slate on which he could map out a new household to replace the first, flawed, arrangement.

Decades later, in 1997 when it became obvious my mother was about to re-enter my life, he repeated the story once more, with a new twist. As a result, it simply wasn't the same story.

There is no explanation for my father's changed story other than that he knew I was about to discover the other side of his tarnished coin and hurriedly attempted to control my opinion. Even if the embarrassment of two of your cousins engaging in a threesome with your wife keeps you from telling the whole truth, it doesn't explain why he said my mother *bragged* about it, or why he later changed his story by saying he wasn't sure if she was raped or not.

I will always be haunted by the pitiful cry, "your daddy hired two men to rape me," that she uttered as I sat at her side for the first time in thirty years.

Unaware of what my father had told me, she said she was assaulted by two of his relatives. The puzzle grew bigger, but it had more missing pieces.

My father says she went horseback riding and was bucked off.

My mother says she needed to go to the store and my father wouldn't take her, so she walked.

Her story is that the two young men, whom she knew well, came along and offered her a ride. She accepted their kindness, hopped into the car, and off they went.

Is it probable that a woman who has recently given birth for the first time would desire sexual gratification so desperately that she neglects her husband, choosing instead to wantonly pleasure his *two* cousins? Would a woman in her vulnerable situation risk losing her standing in church as well as her marriage, along with her son, for whom she had only just traveled from California. It is not plausible that she was a willing participant in sexual misconduct.

And when my father filed for divorce in December, why didn't he say she had committed adultery with his own cousins? This fact alone, most likely, would have guaranteed him an easy divorce and custody of me.

Even after finding my mother, I had little more than a divorced couple's conflicting stories and some tattered bits of circumstantial evidence to go by. Who was I to believe? My father had trained me for decades to fear and doubt my mother. Then when I challenged the status quo, he ruined his own credibility by changing his story for no apparent reason. I churned with confusion until I was finally able to crack the safe containing this darkest of family secrets. What I found was truly odious.

I began by approaching my father's brother, Uncle Ray, and his wife Ruth. They said they remembered that something unpleasant happened on that day. They did not remember, or perhaps declined to acknowledge she was raped, but they did remember who was involved. They recalled only one of the men my father admitted had done the deed. They also informed me that this individual left for California immediately after the incident.

Ruth said my mother walked to the store, and did not recall any horseback riding. My uncle and aunt's version of events already correlated my mother's story more than my father's.

Could his motivation to dump my mother and keep hold of me have been so consuming that he conspired with two relatives to have her raped, accused her of adultery, and then persuaded the same two men to testify before the elders of the Jehovah's Witnesses, saying that she came on to them? Could a man really feel such putrid hate, such contempt for his young, emotionally overloaded wife?

I couldn't leave such an outrage to clandestine family whispers. I had to know, to find the truth. I needed another source—but who else would corroborate either story?

The only candidates were the alleged rapists. After all, it had been forty years; the time allotted by the statute of limitations was firmly in the past. Perhaps they would welcome the opportunity to unload their undoubtedly heavy burden of guilt. Alternatively maybe they would relish the chance to set the record straight regarding my mother's ravenous appetite for unbridled sex.

For months I pondered this. These men are my family; I know their mother. They had grown old and probably enjoyed many grandkids. How would they and the rest of the family react to my questions? This was no easy decision. Even though my father said they had raped my mother forty years ago, I didn't feel it proper to damage their lives; what's done is done. If they were maniacs, maybe they'd try to hurt me or my family in retaliation for digging up long-dead secrets.

A family member issued a memorably ominous warning: "You better be careful. He's crazy!"

But after months of personal reflection, I committed to seek information directly from the alleged culprits, and determined the least invasive approach to be a letter. So I wrote, and I stirred the family pot.

Chapter 14

Don't go believin' what your mother says

The letter was a long shot, I was sure, but if you can't find the courage to light the match, you will never see the fireworks.

I wrote a letter that was intentionally direct and concise, steering well clear of the temptation to vent or preach. I told my second cousin—sincerely—that the past is the past and nothing can change the incident with my mother. The statute of limitations had long since run out and I was not contacting him to accuse or condemn. I asked for a clear yes-or-no answer to the pivotal question:

Was my father involved?

Asking this question felt like pulling the pin on a grenade. I had heard enough family accounts to be convinced there was a foundation of truth. The less straightforward question of whether my mother was a seductress or a rape victim still lingered.

I concluded by stating that if I did not receive a reply, I would not hesitate to pick up the phone. I waited for about a month in a fretful way that felt almost like sitting on prickly pear.

When the reply came, it was not directly from him. My father heard from his cousin before I did.

Eventually I received word through the family grapevine

that my second cousin had been calling around asking about me. He was, quite literally, livid.

It's my understanding his wife got to the letter first. She was, predictably, distressed by such a message; though I took care to compose the letter with as much tact as possible, no amount of etiquette can sweeten something so profoundly bitter.

This unforeseen consequence was nothing like what I had intended. I did not want to singe bystanders as I blazed through a mission of retribution. My business was the truth, not vengeance. My father's cousin, as I heard, was outraged.

"I'll kill him" was the phrase he repeated several times. I was told to guard myself, because he is "unpredictable."

My father, discovering I was meddling in the past, also made a few calls. I half expected family members who were still speaking with me to break off all contact. I was very anxious. My father didn't say much, but what he did say spoke volumes.

At the same moment I believed he would start shouting to our family, *"Lies! All lies!"* Leaving me to explain and defend myself to those who would still speak to me. What he did say was a surprise.

"Bryan's tryin' to dig up some dirt on me," He said.

Upon hearing this, I just gaped. *Why wasn't he calling me a liar?* It suggested acknowledgement that the "dirt" was there to be found. Where was his outrage?

As the dust settled, I waited for some sort of direct response. Neither my father nor the alleged rapist and his wife made contact. Not one person in my family told me to abandon my crazy notions. None of the elders in the family raised a finger to silence my accusations.

My father's cousin would not answer my written inquiry.

Although I hesitated and considered the decision carefully, I knew I had to stick to the assertion that I would telephone him if he did not reply in writing. It was going to have to be my dime.

It took months to build up the courage and resiliency to make this phone call. I was terrified he would scream to the highest peaks, calling me a liar and making threats. I occupied a prison of fear with mortar and bricks supplied by my family. I had an idea of his level of rage, and of how his roots went deep into the coarse sand of central Oklahoma. How dangerous would a man have to be to rape his cousin's wife upon request—if that is what he did?

So, after considering every imaginable angle, I gathered my courage and placed the call. And I spoke to this man.

As with my father, his omissions said as much as many conversations would have. People reveal themselves by saying nothing at all: the gaps, the things left unsaid, reveal shaded meaning beyond the spoken word. Our conversation was short and to the point, but loaded with significant omissions.

"Hello," I said.

"Yeah?" A voice answered.

"Yes. Is Sammy there?" I continued.

"This is he." His rough, nasal, country twang caught me off-guard, weighting the few words he offered. I believe he had lived in California since the *incident*. Even though he spent most of his life on the West Coast, the Heartland was in his back pocket.

"Sammy, this is Bryan McGlothin."

"Yeah. Well I don't want you callin' here no more. And don't go believin' what your mother says."

"Well, it's what my father says too."

"Well, there you go. I don't want you callin' or writin' any-more."

CLICK.

That was it: all he had to say. Or was it?

His first impulse was to attack my mother, ordering me to dismiss her statements: the first line of defense to countless sexual assault accusations. If I had been swayed by this abbreviated denial and doubted her credibility, the crucial evidence was instantly lost.

After he told me not to contact him any further, he could have ended the call without any additional comment. But he was instinctively motivated to defend himself by discrediting my mother.

Then, when I told him my father has said the same as my mother, he made no attempt to challenge my father or me, saying simply, *"well, there you go."*

I had expected him to say something like "your father said no such thing!" Instead his reply was more like "what can I say?" It is the kind of response that indicates shock, resignation, and possibly the gravity of conscience.

I'm left with a strong conviction that I am on the right track. I've discussed it frankly with relatives of each of the people directly involved and yet no-one will call me a liar. No-one has told me to stop my babbling or said I have no respect for my own father. *No-one has denied anything.*

I feel certain several family members know exactly what happened that fateful day, but they're not ready to let the putrid family secret out. If it is true my father induced his cousins to rape his own wife, it would bring an ugly scandal upon the Watchtower as well as the McGlothin name. For my father to have done this as a servant in the Organization and then spend decades as an elder counseling others on their marital problems would certainly show their God was not keeping his house clean, even as they insist Jehovah is always cleansing His Organization. Could it be one evildoer slipped through the grasp of their God?

My father originally claimed she "bragged" she let some guy rape her. But even though she was very young and inexperienced, would she have been so naive as to take a chance on losing custody of her son—and her status as the wife of a servant—by revealing herself as a mindless slut?

And if she did seduce my father's cousins, why didn't he simply file for divorce again there in Oklahoma, on grounds of adultery? It would have been easy for him to attain a scriptural dissolution and gain custody of me if my mother had engaged in such explicit sex with two men at once.

Perhaps he was afraid that, if he introduced the accusation in court, his cousins may get cold feet. He may have been caught in his own web that way. With the Witnesses, what happens in the Kingdom Hall stays in the Kingdom Hall. No-one knows this better than Donald D'Haene.

In his book *Father's Touch,* D'Haene explains how he and his siblings were molested for years by their father. When his father was finally caught and his perversion brought to the attention of the local elders, he was disfellowshipped, but the elders never reported his devious acts to the authorities. The Witnesses take the approach of "let Jehovah take care of it," so his father continued to molest his own children for years afterwards. The remedy given by the elders to most problems in the congregation is to "pray more."

Perhaps my father was willing to play his game in the Kingdom Hall's, dark, judicial room of secrets, where pedophiles and rapists are told to repent and come back in six months? In that back room, my mother was found guilty and, with the blessing of the elders, my father was granted his scriptural divorce. This was all he needed to start his life anew.

To the Jehovah's Witnesses, the distinction between rape and adultery can be a very fine line. Family members on both sides recall my mother being prone to fainting spells. No-one knew why, but it was not uncommon for her to collapse for no apparent reason. My mother knew my father's cousins. If she had accepted their perceived kindness, then realized their true intentions, the stress could have caused her to faint. If this had happened, and she had no way to prove it, it would have been devastating for her.

In cases of rape within the Jehovah's Witness community, the Watchtower says:

> *Such scriptural precedents are applicable to Christians, who are under command, Flee from fornication (1 Cor. 6:18). Thus if a Christian woman does not cry out and does not put forth every effort to flee, she would be viewed as consenting to the violation. The Christian woman who wants to keep clean and obey God's commandments, if faced with this situation today, needs to be courageous and to act on the suggestion made by the Scriptures and scream.*

So even if a woman were to freeze in fear or decide to submit to the terror in order to live to see another day, she still could be found guilty of fornication or adultery. This directive was written by what the Witnesses consider to be "God's appointed channel" here on earth, less than a year before the incident.

This would also explain why, when she went to the

McLoud police, they ignored her pleas for help, because she had no bruises. If she was unconscious, there would be no fight, hence no indication of a struggle.

"I'll beat myself up next time, so they'll take me serious." She later told several family members. I'm sure she felt, as a vulnerable teenaged girl, that the whole world was against her. She was alone, disfellowshipped by what she believed was God's only Organization here on earth, shunned by family and friends, and ignored by the police. She had no-one to turn to and her infant son, once again, was nowhere to be found.

She stayed in the McLoud area for some time, hoping my father would show his face. On March 1st 1965, just three months after my father filed for divorce, my mother filed wife abandonment charges in Lincoln County. A warrant for my father's arrest was filed.

My father had abandoned his wife and stolen their son. They were not divorced. In the suit for legal separation, my father stated he was afraid she would take me out of the state, and then fled with me to an out-of-state location: Louisville, Kentucky.

"I don't believe his lawyer got a letter from Kentucky," my Aunt wrote.

Child abduction laws did not exist in their current form at that time, but nevertheless, my father had taken me out of state twice without my mother's knowledge. She had left with me once to go to California, after saying a straightforward goodbye to her husband. This is far from what he had indoctrinated in me for decades.

She searched for me for months; laying low, getting waitress jobs near McLoud and Harrah as well in the area of the Tinker Air Force base. She began a letter writing campaign, mailing them to my grandparents, Buck and Lucille. They would then forward her letters to my father in Kentucky:

> *Dear Lucille and all,*
>
> *I received a letter from Freddie and baby. Although they have been sick. Freddie sent me a picture of Bryan and he is so cute. And he sure had grown. I've written Freddie another letter. Would you mail it as soon as you can?*
> *Take care and tell hello to everyone for me.*
> *As ever*
>
> *Angie.*

The communication was not dated, but the envelope, mailed from El Monte, California, was dated January 24th 1966; I was eighteen months old. I believe this letter from my mother wore my father down, because two months later, my mother and I would be reunited.

Chapter 15

To see him reared outside Jehovah's Organization

My father moved with me to Kentucky and he nestled us into the community of Louisville. He became a servant once again in a local congregation.

"Well, I gave my talk again Sunday. Sure do enjoy giving them," he wrote to his parents. He continues with news that I have been sick: "Bryan had that virus Saturday [night]..."

Concerned with his hours of preaching door to door, he continues: "I went into service Saturday afternoon & Sunday morning. Hoping to build my time up."

Whether influenced by guilt, sympathy, loneliness, expressed threats, or the sheer burden of single parenthood, he allowed my mother back into our home.

I was only eighteen months old and therefore have no recollection, but I do have a letter from my father to the Watchtower. In the correspondence he is inquiring whether or not he still has his scriptural divorce after taking my mother into his home and, I'm assuming, having sex with her. The letter is dated March 13th 1967:

> *I have written you previously concerning my wife, Angie McGlothin. In the last letter I received, you did state that I had grounds for a scriptural divorce. However, she acted like she was ready to straiten up, so I*

took her back on March 12th 1966.

The reasons my father allowed my mother back may not be known, but she had plans of her own:

She stayed only nine days, taking our son with her.
He had been staying with me while we were separated.

On March 21st, my mother sold several pieces of my father's camera equipment and purchased a plane ticket to Orlando, Florida, where her sister, Sherry, and brother-in-law, Eddie, had moved. Sherry says my mother showed up with me in a little brown suit.

"You looked so cute," she mused.

This was the first time my mother had taken me without my father's knowledge. She apparently decided she could play the same game as he. Regardless of the morality of her action, it is the opposite of what my father told me for years. She expected him to follow her to Southern California, so she took me to Florida first.

Returning to the El Monte area after visiting my aunt and uncle, my mother attempted to create a normal life for us. She found work near Lillie's home. Lillie would baby-sit me during the week and my mother would ride her bike to Lillie's for lunch each day, so that we could enjoy "Mom's" home cooking together. This was where my mother took the pictures of me on the sofa. She also had several pictures taken of me around this time. It's so peculiar to see photos of myself as a toddler in her home. I didn't retain even the slightest memory of that time; I know it only through pictures and stories. This is also the time during which Jack says he used to take me everywhere.

"We were like buddies," he told me.

It was during this period that they took me to spend the weekend on the Colorado River, and let me run about "butt naked," as Jack put it, to air out a diaper rash.

Lillie told my mother to file for divorce to stop my father from taking me away once again. Just as she had once rebelled against her mother-in-law's advice to give me extra water, my mother refused to heed Lillie's counsel. She was only a teenager and still growing out of her rebellious streak. She had already traveled across the country more than once to find and keep her son. I can't begin to imagine what her life was like.

My father soon made an unsuccessful trip to El Monte. He told me how he grew a mustache and dyed his hair red. He saw my mother walking to our trailer house there in the park with "some man." Perhaps fear of confrontation with someone other than a teenage girl prevented him from abducting me again. Alone, she was an easy target for my father. Jack says he's almost certain when this took place. He remembers walking us home one evening. We were going out for dinner, but mom had run out of diapers for me. On the way from Jack's parents' home, he was holding my hand as we walked the two hundred yards back to the trailer. He remembers me whipping my head around to look at a guy we passed on the sidewalk.

"Maybe you recognized him," Jack told me.

My great-grandmother, Angie Leslie Turner, told my father where I was on at least one occasion. Both my father and mother say this. Other family members feel there is no way Angie Turner would have done this to her own granddaughter. They were too close and Angie Turner adored my mother. Jack, who has firsthand knowledge, says their relationship was not always as warm as it seemed to others.

"Your momma told me she hated Angie Turner for a while," He said.

After the last time my father took me, Jack drove my mother to the trailer park where her father and second wife, Belen, lived. They didn't travel there to visit her father; Angie Turner lived in that same court. My mother was angry with her grandmother and felt she had to confront her about she had done.

"I stayed in the car," Jack said. "I didn't want no part of that!"

My mother marched into her grandmother's trailer and did not come out for some time. When she did return, her demeanor was no different. Angie Turner soon moved to Sacramento, California, and my mother did not attempt to visit her again until her death.

As Angie Turner lay on her deathbed, my mother and her cousin, Judy, arrived in Sacramento with no accommodation. Their aunts, Georgia Lee and Vera, had already secured a hotel room and my mother and Judy were allowed to share the room for one night.

Vera, a Jehovah's Witness, told my mother to leave the next day; my mother was still disfellowshipped. Judy and my mother pooled their money and found their own room. Judy refused to abandon my mother as so many family members had already done.

I don't understand how my great-grandmother, Angie Turner, could turn against my mother in such a horrific way, but as a young boy, it made sense to me. My father told me that my mother's own grandmother told him where we were because my mother was living such a debauched life. This only came together recently when I discovered Angie Turner was a Jehovah's Witness.

Her viewpoint, like all Witnesses, was that a child out of the Watchtower is a dead child. My mother was still cast out from Jehovah's Organization and probably, after her experience, wanted nothing more to do with them. Even though she did try to regain her fellowship and family within the Organization, she was still a *worldly* person in their eyes: one who had turned her back on *their* Jehovah.

She attended several meetings, but just couldn't take sitting in the back, and being stared at but not spoken to. One thing is for certain: the Watchtower comes before family. This is probably why Angie Turner turned on her own granddaughter.

My mother's elation at having me back in her life was short lived. In his letter to the Watchtower Society, my father takes up the sequence of events:

> *In September 1966, I went to California to get my son back as I just couldn't stand to see him reared outside Jehovah's Organization.*

This is the event with which we began my story: my father pretending to be in pain, then as my mother goes into the store, speeding off in the car with me.

My father's statement that he "couldn't stand to see [me] reared outside Jehovah's Organization" is a testament to the belief of the Witnesses that they alone are God's people, and all others will be destroyed at Armageddon. They are a Doomsday cult, believing that their reward comes only when God destroys all others.

He continues the letter by providing two witnesses that enable the Watchtower to judge her guilty of the sin of adultery:

> *Two of Angie's friends told me that Angie was living with a man. The day I got my son, I spent the afternoon with Angie and she told me she was living with this man and had been for over a year, off and on. She said she was living with him when she came back to me on March 12th 1966. She said she only came back to get the baby.*

I don't doubt the statement that my mother "only came back to get the baby." She was desperate to get her child back, and if she had to use deception, then so be it.

My father's letter then states that we are once again together and attending the Kingdom Hall in Louisville, Kentucky. What he says next is very telling:

> *Brothers what I want now is a divorce and most of all custody of my son, so she won't get him again. I can get a divorce and custody on grounds of desertion. Angie's whereabouts is unknown, so she would not contest the divorce.*

This, I feel is the whole reason my father didn't stick around to finalize the divorce in Oklahoma. Now he had my mother where he wanted her: gone. It was ridiculous to claim that her whereabouts were unknown. He knew where many of her family members lived in both California and Arizona. After all, my mother's grandmother tracked her down for him on one occasion.

On the way back from California in July 1964, when my mother didn't want to return to Oklahoma, we stayed at her grandparents' home in Merana, Arizona. They still lived in the same house when my father filed for divorce in Louisville. The law in Kentucky, though, was that if the defendant was at an unknown location, the requirements for a suit in their absence were a notice published in the local paper and a letter to convey information to the last known address. She was never told she was being sued for divorce and she had no idea she was to lose custody of her only child and receive no order for visitation.

My father closes his letter with humble words of devotion:

Jehovah's Organization is all I have to hold on to now and I certainly want my son and me to be in that new system of things..."

As a servant, he knew the system and worked it well. He had a plan and all he had to do was be patient. It would not be long at all before the "Brothers" in Brooklyn would reply. His whole scheme relied on their willingness to accept his word over actual evidence. He waited, and I'm sure he prayed.

Chapter 16

I was not to blame and I am without fault

The Watchtower replied to my father with what I consider to be the most absurd reasoning possible. They write:

You indicate that you took your wife, Angie, back on March 12, 1966. However, she stayed only nine days and left, taking your son with her. This has been while she was in a disfellowshipped state and, as we understand matters, she is still disfellowshipped.

If this is true and she confessed to you that she has been living in adultery since the time you last had sexual relations with her, you could present this information to the congregation committee, filing a written, signed statement witnessed by a member of the committee with the congregation as to this matter.

Your conscience would then be charged with the responsibility for the decision that establishes the adulterous grounds for the divorce in this instance.

Then if you obtain a divorce on any legal grounds, providing of course the committee accepts the evidence of adultery you present to them, the committee would not take any action against you if you were to subsequently remarry.

Telling my father, in effect, that "you write whatever you want and get it signed and we'll let you have your scriptural divorce" was like giving Mad Dog 20/20 to a drunk. This final letter gave my father the go-ahead for his legal divorce and claim for custody. I suppose that, since my mother was forced out of the Watchtower, she didn't have the right to defend herself. She was found guilty of adultery once again, though this time *in absentia* and without evidence. There was no need for the two-witness rule this time, because my father said she did it—just as he told me she had died.

He filed for divorce in Jefferson County, Kentucky, on April 3rd 1967. In the suit he never mentions my mother taking me out of the state without his knowledge, even though it would have cast an even darker shadow upon her. However, if he had, he would also have had to explain to the court his abduction of me in California. He said:

Yes, the defendant abandoned me here in Louisville, KY on March 12th 1966 and has not lived with me since that time. She took off, without my knowing she was going to leave, and she pawned some of the things that belonged to me and took the money and I have never got it back. She left the city of Louisville, KY and I learned she is living with another man."

He also omits that she was there, in his home, for only nine days. He continues:

I was not to blame and I am without fault...I worked and supported her and the child and tried to please her and to get along but nothing did any good.

For nine long days, he provided for my mother there in Kentucky, but she couldn't be satisfied. My father obviously had it all well thought out. In the suit, he gives an address for my mother, which I have not been able to connect to her. In fact, the required letter sent to that address, informing her she was being sued for divorce, was returned. It was returned with the stamp, "Addressee Unknown," and the handwritten words, "no such name, not known," as if my mother had never been there. She may have lived there: I don't know. I do know that today there is no Chandler St. in Monterey Park. There is a North Chandler Avenue. Could it be the same? One thing is certain; my father knew how to contact plenty of my mother's relatives, any of whom probably could have told him the whereabouts of twenty-year-old Angie McGlothin. But that would not have served his purpose.

As sly as my father was, he was not quick enough. My mother was still waiting, and she had a surprise for him.

Although my father had told me, when I was a young boy, of the time my mother had him arrested, it was Aunt Anna Marie who gave me the full account.

Looking back, I think my aunt may have felt differently about my family's conniving to keep me hidden from my mother. Or perhaps it was sympathy for me that prompted her to save my mother's personal things until I grew older. She was the only family member to enlighten me with such a detailed account of the incident in which my father landed in jail on Thanksgiving Day, 1967.

My father had traveled to McLoud on the holiday week-end with me and his girlfriend, Ina Jo, and her kids, Kathy and Carrie. Jo would soon become my stepmother. He had, as my aunt put it, "come to show off his girlfriend." None of my family has ever been much of a Jo fan.

My mother had not laid eyes on me in approximately four-teen months, and she was hiding out in the McLoud area, waiting to spot my father and me. This, she thought, was her lucky day. She had filed "wife abandonment" charges against my father earlier, in July in Oklahoma County. Whether the authorities or my mother spotted my father, the fireworks were lit.

Police lights shot through the windows of my grandparent's home. Cuffs were applied to my father's wrists as my mother went running around the house searching for an open window; she knew I had to be close by. The police questioned my father as to my whereabouts as my mother tested each pane.

"I don't know," He replied as the police pushed him into the patrol car.

My mother was energized when a window gave way, slamming it against the top of the casement. She sprang immediately through the window, hands on the floor and feet still in the dirt.

Everyone in the house had spotted her circling the house and my aunt was prepared. My mother put one knee on the windowsill and Aunt Anna Marie appeared with a broom raised over her head like a major leaguer.

"If you don't get outta here, I'm gonna knock the shit outta ya!" She threatened.

My mother didn't think twice. She removed herself from the window, satisfied my father would be in jail through the holiday weekend, unable to take flight with me.

"The amazing thing was," my aunt said, "we had put you under the bed, and you slept though the whole thing."

I was three-and-a-half years old, hidden under my grand-parents' bed, with the yard filled with police lights and people yelling, and I slept through the entire incident.

The next day, my mother filed for divorce and temporary custody, hoping to gain guardianship of me. The suit not only says my father abandoned her over a year prior, but also includes my grandparents as accomplices:

> *That by stealth, deceit, and chicanery the defendants, Freddie Lee McGlothin, Buck McGlothin and Lucille McGlothin have conspired to deprive the plaintiff of her minor child and that a temporary order should issue against these defendants and all of them, compelling them to deliver the child into the custody of its mother, the plaintiff herein.*

My mother's accusation that my grandparents conspired with my father is correct. The only contact she had with my father was through them. Then, when my father was arrested and my mother tried so hard to get into their house, they were hiding me under their bed. Not that I blame them, really. What mother or father would not fight for their son and grandson? Their bias understandably clouded their judgment.

My mother's accusation of abandonment in July, earlier that year, was a grave mistake. She did something that hurt her case against my father; she lied. My father saved two newspaper clips from this incident. The first clip reads:

Wife Says Mate Hid Child

A divorce action was filed Monday in district court against a Lincoln County man accused of physically kicking his wife from a car and concealing the couple's small child from her for nearly three years.

My mother lied. I'm certain from all the documents and letters I've seen, that my father never kicked her from a car. She probably said this to make the abduction seem even worse, in an attempt to gain more sympathy and support. She didn't need to lie. The charge of concealing me was plenty.

There was another big problem. My mother filed charges in Oklahoma County. The incident of which she spoke would have happened in Lincoln County. This left the Oklahoma County with no jurisdiction. The next news clip says it all:

Charge By Wife Dismissed

A wife abandonment charge filed in Oklahoma County against a Lincoln County man has been dismissed. The charge, filed last July 20, named Freddie Lee McGlothin, whose wife signed a complaint alleging McGlothin physically kicked her from a car, and had hidden their small child from her since that time.

Story Changed

District Attorney Curtis P. Harris said the criminal action against McGlothin was dropped when the wife, on later questioning by the prosecutors, changed her story.

He said she claimed the alleged kicking incident happened at a spot beyond the Oklahoma-Lincoln County Line, and that this district would have no jurisdiction. In addition Harris said Mrs. Angie Lenora McGlothin admitted allegations she made against McGlothin were not all together factual.

I feel she combined the story of my father speeding off with me in the car in California in September '66 with his running to Kentucky with me in January '65, and added a little more drama. My father was quite proud when he gave me the clippings, telling me they proved she was a liar and pointing out how the charge was dropped. There is one other, overriding, reason for the dismissal, on which my father did not comment. The fact that my mother lied had no bearing on the case. The fact that whatever happened took place out of the jurisdiction of Oklahoma County made no difference either.

Although my mother filed for divorce just after my father was arrested, she didn't know that my father's had already divorced her secretly—in Kentucky just three months earlier. That court had already given my father custody of me, with a legal divorce to go along with his scriptural divorce from the Watchtower Society. The hands of the Oklahoma court were tied and my father was free to remarry.

Soon after his arrest, my father was released on bail. He obtained a copy of his divorce on December 5th and proudly showed up for his Oklahoma County court date of December 8th, providing the judge with his coveted divorce papers. What a shock it must have been for my mother when he made his last move, tossing her final piece from the board.

To her shock, she was no longer married and had no visitation rights with her own son. The charges were thrown out of the Oklahoma court and my father wed my stepmother three days later, on the 11th. It was *check and mate*. My father put the final nail to my mother's coffin and enjoyed wielding the hammer. She was left financially and emotionally broken, barred from her only child. A beaten woman, she traveled back to California where she resigned to the fact that this was simply her life. She returned several times to Oklahoma to find me. I'm told one time she actually hitchhiked the entire trip. Each time though, none of my family had a good word for her. No-one would help me reunite with my mother; she was no longer one of them because she was disfellowshipped.

At this point, for fear of my mother catching up with him, and perhaps taking further legal action, my father began moving, along with his new family, from state to state. Beginning with Indiana, we continued to travel, moving nearly every twelve months, for close to five years.

Finally, my father felt we could settle down in Kemah, Texas. I was in third grade. My mother continued to write letters to my father, through his parents, until at least June 23rd 1972. Her final pleading letter reveals how beaten down she had become, begging to know if her son had decent teeth, if he was tall, if he knew who she was.

This letter reveals a great deal concerning my father's character: his arrogance and disregard of my mother's pleas, and what he did to me.

I now know that when he asked if I knew Jo was not my mother, explaining to me that my own mother was demonized; the time when I was fifteen and told him I wanted to find my mother, and he said she bragged to him that she let "some guy" rape her; in 1982, when I was an adult about to wed and told him I wanted to invite my mother and he informs me of her death by overdose; at all those times and in response to all my queries, that letter was in his bedroom closet. And my mother's address was on that letter. She lived there from when I was six until I turned twenty.

If he had shared the address with me within a year of receiving it, I'm sure my mother would not have attempted suicide. Even after I became an adult, my father lied to me and hid the letter, its contents, and the address. Yet he had the gall to call my mother a conniver and a liar, all the while hiding the information I needed to find her.

"Fred, it was such a long time between letters, could you write more often? Please?" She begged him.

With this letter in his possession he told me, "Don't you think if your momma wanted anything to do with you, she would've already found you?" His words leave a putrid tang in my mouth as I think of my mother's plea: "Please let me know how Bryan is doing from time to time." I am sickened by what he did to his young wife, and to me, his own son. A supposed Christian leader of a supposed Christian sect, he spewed lies and hatred to his own blood, drowning me in bile. All the while my mother chokes on her own heartbreak, and finally gives up on seeing the rising sun, much less the face of her own son.

My father put himself on a pedestal; made my mother his footstool and me his puppet. All he had to do was pull the strings and I responded. I was a little child; of course I believed. He must have felt like such a big man.

My mother was betrayed and beaten. She was alone and had no clue how to carry on. She seemed to ricochet like a pinball, reacting erratically to every motion around her. From what I have gleaned from family, she became irrational, and lived her life as if tomorrow would not come, much as I did after leaving the Watchtower. She became weary of the fight and gave up on life, despaired of her dream of family and child.

But she never lost her beauty. It was the only strength she had—and she used it, from romping in the night with men she'd just met, to assorted affairs. It was almost as if she wanted to succeed at the worst possible deeds. Having tried to live the life taught to her as "God's way," and being burned to her very core, she gave up with no reward.

In the late sixties, she married a man named Rich, who had several children. The marriage lasted only a number of weeks or months before she divorced him.

"All he wanted was a baby-sitter." She said.

Once again she had made a wrong turn and continued on her zigzag path, being pushed this way and that.

Through this time, she and Jack, her longtime friend, had dated off and on. In fact, Jack's family was the only safe harbor she had in her life. On Saturday, March 21st 1970, they finally tied the knot in Las Vegas, in the Courthouse Chapel across from the Clark County Courthouse. Unknown to her, I lived in Fayetteville, Arkansas, and was about to start first grade. I had no clue who she was or even that she was missing.

She decided to put all the late night trysts and toxic bottles behind her and anchor to the steady mooring of Jack and his family. This union probably seemed the only stable thing in my mother's life and though she carried an enormous amount of emotional baggage, Jack loved her dearly.

At about the same time, his parents moved to East Oklahoma. Jack recalls traveling to visit them twice. He said my mother would take the car ninety miles to McLoud and drive by the old places, looking for any sign of her son, hoping to see me in the front yard of my grandparent's home, playing under the Catalpa trees. I was never there, and she never forgot.

The marriage was filled with separations as my mother was unable to subdue her restlessness. Whether she felt too close to the earth or realized it was too stable for her blood, I may never know.

She left Jack and began dating her boss, who was married

with children. She was looking for the happiness she would never attain. She was looking to be bad to appease her guilt. She was driving her speeding car through LA, daring the lights to turn red. And they did.

Chapter 17

It was Tuesday, July 13ᵗʰ 1973

My mother had moved into her own apartment and was set. She was decorating: hanging wallpaper, getting ready for her new life. Her boss had bought her a new wardrobe, and a 1964 Grand Prix.

Once again, my mother's search for happiness had led her down a steep, dark road of nothingness. This time there would be no retreat, no fork in the road. When the day came for him to leave his family and bless my mother with the elusive joy and love she had searched for all her life, he backed out. He told her he could not leave his home.

She was devastated.

She took her prescriptions of Valium and Vicodin, and soaked the toxic mix in vodka. Crawling into the corner, she called her lover and explained that she was on the way out for good. He called her landlord, who knew my mother was in a bad way, and told her to check on the distraught woman.

When the landlord knocked on the door, there was no answer. The landlord unbolted the lock and found my mother huddled in the corner, unconscious. She had grown weary and chosen to sleep instead, or perhaps to start over. It was Tuesday, July 13ᵗʰ 1973.

I was nine years old and on my summer break. I had just attended the International Assembly of Jehovah's Witnesses in the Astrodome. I was probably fishing on the pier at Clear Lake at the end of Lakeside Drive, dreaming of better days. Perhaps I was attempting to deduce, if my mother was truly demonized, what the odds were that I was as well.

I hadn't a clue how hard she had fought for me, and how much she truly loved me. I never knew about the pleading letters she had sent my father, begging to see me.

She was in a coma for six weeks. Jack came back into her life, visiting her daily in the hospital. He told his parents she was not expected to live, and that if she ever woke up, she would never live a normal life.

Lillie and William traveled back to California to be with their daughter-in-law. Lillie never gave up on the daughter she never had. She would hold Angie's hand and talk to her constantly.

One day, while my mother was hooked up to an EEG machine to monitor brain activity, Lillie announced that she was leaving for the cafeteria.

The inked needles began to weave and bounce in excitement. Lillie frantically called the nurses and revealed the thoughts my sleeping mother was hiding. The brain waves were so strong the doctors disconnected the machine because the needles were colliding, greedily searching for white space.

It was late August when my mother awoke from her sleep. Though alive, she had severely damaged her brain. After swallowing her venomous cocktail, she stopped breathing long enough that brain cells began dying off one after another. She suffocated in her own home, alone as she had been for much of her life.

Jack remained by her side after she awoke. He visited her throughout therapy and brought her home. He taught her to speak and eat again, to hold a fork and walk. He was always there, and always has been for over thirty-three years. He truly loved her and still does. That anchor was always there for my mother to take hold.

Chapter 18

Parental abduction is child abuse

It seemed a lifetime for my mother, no doubt. I lived it as well. Each fall she listened to the geese overhead, and each spring she enjoyed the perfume of new flowers in the garden.

There were only two constants in her life: Jack caring for her day to day, and her son's absence, day after day. As twin souls lost in the cosmos we longed for each other; dreaming of that day, burgeoning with undeniable exuberance, along with the fear of disheartened rejection.

My father poured fuel onto both our fears. My mother was certain he was infusing my young mind with evil lies of her wickedness, as often told by feuding parents. Of course I can attest to the truth and the lies. I have seen both sides of the road. I lived on that street for decades, and feel as though I have been struck more than once.

For years Jack says, my mother would ask, "If my boy loves me, why don't he come and find me?"

Unknown to her, I was traveling closer and closer every day. It just took a few decades to find the right house, the right door.

Perhaps one of the greatest tragedies was the indifference of those who could have brought us together even before she attempted suicide; those ones preaching from door to door. They knew of the man among their own ranks who had abducted a mother's child in stealth, and they turned a blind eye. For this is Theocratic Warfare: the giving of information only to those deserving of it. My mother, no longer a Witness, was not deserving. Had these Jehovah's Witnesses wanted to help, I could have been found within days.

In his research paper, "Lying in Court and Religion: An Analysis of the Theocratic Warfare Doctrine of the Jehovah's Witnesses," Jerry Bergman, Ph.D. writes:

> *The Watchtower teaches that lying to "God's ene-mies" is not really lying but theocratic "war strategy" and that "God's Word commands: 'Speak truth each of you with his neighbor' (Eph. 4:25). This command, however, does not mean that we should tell everyone who asks us all he wants to know. We must tell the truth to one who is entitled to know, but if one is not so enti-tled we may be evasive."*
>
> *The latest discussion appeared in the February 8th 2000 issue of* Awake! *which, under the title "Cautious as Serpents," notes:*
>
> *"Of course, being truthful does not mean that we are obligated to divulge all information to anyone who asks it of us."*
>
> *The Watchtower has its own definition of lying:*
>
> > LIE: *The opposite of truth. Lying generally involves saying something false to a person who is entitled to know the truth and doing so with the intent to deceive or injure him or another person."*

My mother was not "entitled to know" the location of her son because she was no longer a Jehovah's Witness. By refus-ing to help her, they revealed their true nature. For they believe if you are not one of them, you are a dead person, living on the coattails of Satan.

Looking back now, it amazes me how the actions of my father—one man—could have done so much damage. I feel damaged. My mother is damaged. Even if he did not force her to attempt suicide, by forcing her to live without the son she carried inside her, he certainly influenced her life in that direction.

I have grown jealous of those who have, or at least who know, both their parents. I am astonished that some adults make decisions, using their children, to punish other adults they once loved.

I wish I could know what it's like to truly be happy for extended periods of time. Real joy eludes me. Though I am free of the fear once instilled in me by the Watchtower, depression continually knocks at my door. I cannot lay my head on my pillow and go back to a time of fond memories of family. Reminiscing about my young days does not bring a smile to my face. Jealousy of my wife and others as they recall childhood events as euphoric experiences plagues me. I quiet my mind and concentrate. I ask myself, what did we do together? The words *love* and *proud* never came from my father's lips. Instead, my memory throws out insults like "half mentally retarded," and "the most forgetful kid I ever seen."

"You get that from your mother," he'd say harshly. His touch was foreign to me, other than in a rage against my flesh. I often wondered: *If I'm so bad, why don't you let me go back to my mother?*

But in his mind, to reunite us would have been to let her win. My father was playing a high-stakes game and I was his ace. He manipulated my very being as his own plaything in a torturous game. And in the end, no-one won.

Though I've spent most of my life in this cramped room devoid of light, I know I'm not here alone. We shift in and out of the space as we muddle our way through, not knowing in which direction our emotions will swing tomorrow, and we do our best to live to the fullest today.

This is not to say there is no happiness in my life. I have found my mother along with my peace of mind. My unbelievable wife warms my heart. Yet this doesn't stop the demons from returning: those painful memories: the thoughts of *what if?*

At times I feel as though my whole life has been stolen from me, wasted on the whim of a cultic fanatic set on being one-up on his ex. How might I be different if I had been allowed to experience the love of a mother as a child? What if I had been able to play in sports in high school, run for class president, have friends who accepted me for who I was and not because I attended their place of worship? How would my life differ if I had been encouraged to seek higher education? Would I feel closer to my family if I had warm memories of Christmas, of the glowing smiles on my parents' faces as I stripped the wrapping from my new train? If I'd had my mother's love and warm affections yesterday, would I be more emotionally stable today? And if so, would I have been a better father myself? Would I be a better son?

These are the demons from below which visit me unannounced: the memories, the what-ifs, along with the reality of my life. To say I am thankful to have found my mother would be an understatement. Her presence is healing to my soul. Just knowing she is happier because I found her, gives me great joy. Yet no matter how much time I spend with her, no matter how many phone calls and Holidays we share, I will never truly know who my mother was. She is a shell of her former self.

When I visit her I ask how she's doing, if she's treating Jack well, and keeping him in line. She giggles and gives me her quick answers, looking at me then to the floor every two or three seconds. She laughs and rocks, then returns her gaze to her television show. For this is her life; she lives in her chair, watching TV from when she awakes until when she retires for the night. She flips her long, grey, Cherokee locks as her eyes dart the room.

"It's funny to hear 'mom,'" She tells me over and over in rapid succession until I acknowledge her.

The anger on her face is evident as her lips will not form the words she wants to convey. At times, as an older sibling translates for the younger, Jack tells me what she is trying to say. He has been at her side, after all, for over thirty-three years. She says Jack is her best friend.

"He's my knight!" She tells me.

Not only is he her savior, but he is my angel. I shudder to think where she would be today were it not for him. My mother did not always show Jack the love and devotion he desired from her, though he was always there when she returned after losing her way. He certainly has more love flowing through his veins than my father. Jack has spent a lifetime loving my mother, more than my father loved his own son.

"Well, I hope you two are happy together" were my father's last bitter words to me.

He has not spoken to me in almost nine years; not that I'm dying to converse with him. Life is just so ironic at times: spending my life searching for my mother only to lose my father, all in the name of God.

"That makes you an Apostate," He told me.

"I can't associate with you." He said.

And this is true according to the teachings of the Watchtower. Leaving their church is second only to being the Antichrist; committing such a sin will leave you without family and friend, not to mention the years it requires deprogramming.

Having fled the Watchtower a decade ago, one would think my mother and I would be free of its emotional blackmail. Unfortunately, that is not the case. We have not truly escaped the massive Watchtower. To my own sorrow, my daughter has joined the ranks of those who deny their own family.

Just one year ago, after her nineteenth birthday, she took a stand against her own flesh as prescribed by the Watchtower Organization. At her last visit just a month earlier, I had not scolded her nor struck her. I was not a drunk, nor did I abuse her in any way. I did however reveal to her a truth: that the Watchtower Bible and Tract Society Inc. had been a *Non-governmental member of the United Nations* for almost ten years. This may seem trivial to most people, but those who have been associated with the Witnesses know the depth of this hypocrisy.

For decades, since the United Nations began as the League of Nations, the Watchtower has taught that the U.N. is none other than the Scarlet Wild Beast spoken of in Revelations. The May 1st 1999 issue of the Watchtower states:

> *Subsequently, its December 15th 1929 issue, the Watchtower issued the definitive statement that the "whole tendency of the League of Nations is to turn the people away from God and from Christ, and it is therefore a desolating thing, the product of Satan, and an*

abomination in the sight of God." In time, the League, held by the Watchtower Society to be a "desolating thing," gave way to the United Nations.

Jehovah's Witnesses have long exposed these human peace organizations as disgusting in God's sight: "This beast is supported by world rulers... as a peace organization that came into existence in 1919 as the League of Nations. That is now the United Nations." Yet the Watchtower affiliated itself with the United Nations, which they firmly believe is a "product of Satan." Having been taught for decades of the evils which lie in the U.N., it is unfathomable that the teachers themselves would form an alliance with it, especially when a member of the congregation is threatened with being disfellowshipped if he were to join the YMCA to use the gym.

The January 1st 1979 issue of *The Watchtower* magazine speaks of this same fact in "Questions from Readers:"

Hence, for one of Jehovah's Witnesses to become a member of such a so-called "Christian" association would amount to apostasy.

My phone calls went unanswered for over a month after I finally received my daughter's dreadful words. To say her letter was not heartbreaking would be to say fire is not painful:

Although you are my father, we have chosen different paths. You have chosen the world, and not to live by Bible principles or standards. You disassociated yourself, and you chose what you wanted to do. You know enough about the Witnesses to know that I should treat you like a disfellowshipped person...I feel that associat-

202

ing with you is a [hindrance] to my spirituality.

The Witnesses label everyone who is not a Witness as being "of the *world.*" And those "of the world" do not carry the same spiritual strength as they. In their eyes we are people who will be destroyed, very soon, by God's mighty hand in Armageddon.

I would feel a lot better with myself if I didn't associate with you. Because I should treat you like a disfellowshipped person. So basically until you start doing something about the truth, I don't want to be around you, or talk to you. Because I don't want to, nor do I need to.

Once again, the shunning policy of even family members by the Watchtower has plagued my house. Because I have chosen not to believe as she, I am labeled an Apostate and am rejected and shunned until I return to her "truth." She finishes her hateful words with the revelation of an upcoming wedding.

I am also engaged to a Brother. I don't want him to meet you, or talk to you because you are not good association. And I don't think you should come to my wedding, because I do not want an apostate at my wedding. He also has an understanding about this, because he has 2 disfellowshipped brothers. You brought this upon yourself, and for that I am sorry, because you cannot truly be happy with your life, unless you have Jehovah and the congregation backing you up. So here is where we must part. If you wish to

contact me, I would prefer you write me a letter, or an
email, because I won't be taking your phone calls.

She closes her cold letter along with a portion of her father's heart. To have lost so much in life, family and friend, joy and peace to one cultish organization is unimaginable. Yet each time I speak with my mother she inquires of her beautiful "grandbaby."

"She's doing fine Mom," I tell her.

I see no need to break her heart once again. Mine is sufficient for us both.

Even as my loving mother has returned to my life, the worn gears of my existence continues to grind my damaged psyche. The damage my father inflicted in me in the name of God is evident.

In her report, "Parental Kidnapping: A New Form of Child Abuse," Nancy Faulkner, Ph.D. writes:

Lowell Streicker, the director of the freedom Counsel-
ing Center in Burlingame, brings up the issue of a spe-
cial group of child stealing victims whose parents are
involved in a religious organization, possibly a cult.
One parent may also perceive the other as being the
enemy of the true faith and that parent conceives that
the eternal salvation of the child depends on "rescu-
ing" the child from the parent who is not in the reli-
gious group. The return of the child is complicated by
the child's experience in the cult group. These children
appear to be confused, disoriented, and in addition,
seem to have internalized some sense of the parent per-
petrator's paranoid fantasies about the evil doings of
the outside society.

Though my father may have used his godly viewpoints as an excuse for my abduction, I feel sure it was more a case of power over the weak. I was unable to defend myself, as was my mother. My father was not a hero for my cause. He was a child abuser.

Faulkner continues:

> *The children become "emotional dishrags" because the perpetrator tells the child that the parent victim doesn't want them anymore, doesn't love them anymore, that the parent victim is dead, or may be getting married and doesn't want them around. The older children (ages 8 or 9) are pressured more heavily by the perpetrator to form a negative image of the parent victim, probably to assure that the child will not attempt to contact the parent victim.*

Just how long those who love me can weather my rough seas, I continue to speculate. At forty-one years old I still feel a victim. My mother has blessed my life now for close to eight years and still yet I feel there is little healing.

Again, Dr. Faulkner reveals a truth I know all too well as an adult victim of child abduction:

> *In the future, the children feel distrustful of people, have a hard time falling in love, hard time letting go, and feel very vulnerable for many years. One must look always at the very long term effects (one of our interviewed victims had been stolen twenty-five years before, and she said, "I have a feeling like I was lost in time and space," because she moved so much and went to so many different schools. She still does not feel normal).*

Normal. Yes, I have long yearned to know normal. Those around me over these last few years have given me a glimpse of the world of normality; no-one more so that the ever-patient woman who shares her life with mine. Were it not for her, I might not have been writing these words at this moment. Just as Jack has been the anchor of my mother's life, so has my blessed wife, Evelyne, brought peace and stability to mine.

As a child clutches her favorite doll by its frayed clothes or tangled hair, she hangs on to me and my insanity, every day trying harder to understand the tormented man she loves dearly. Incredibly, she has brought me the love I had sought for many decades. Nothing on the planet offers the sense of peace and joy of a true, unconditional, loving relationship.

Though I lost my daughter to the cultic teachings of the Watchtower, I do hold out hope that she, as I, will one day wake up and realize God does not require us to disown family and friend just because they do not believe as we do. I look forward to that time of reunion just as I did with my mother.

Even in my darkest days I realize I am not alone. Hundreds of thousands of children are the victims of parental kidnap every year. We huddle in the darkness as we are thrown about, trained to hate and fear. Our desires become secondary as we submit to the overwhelming force of the masters of the game. We are dangled as trophies for the loser to covet. We are the unwitting daggers thrust into the backs of the ones we love, the ones judged as evil. We are the ones in the dark who never speak of our own truth for fear our only happiness, our mind's fantasies, may be judged evil as well, for we may be misplaced in the void, but we still have the beauty of our inner thought, and the hope of one day finding our own happiness.

In my first words to my mother:

I think a great tragedy in life is living yours in the shadows of the decisions that others make.

We desire and need guidance from those we trust. When they instead lead us to the slaughter, we are emotionally skinned and our tender psyches cast about. As children we are held captive and controlled by fear. And as adults we carry the scars to our very end.

We travel to the moon and Mars. Search the starry skies and hollow out holes in the earth to disco ver from whence we have come. It is that curiosity, in the innermost parts of our mind,that keeps us searching for our origins.

Though much work has been done to understand the impact of child abduction, little study has been done to understand the implication of parental abduction. Some feel that because the child is abducted by a parent, that the child in not in harm's way. As you can see from my tragic story, this is a false assumption.

If you are currently a victim of parental abduction, there is help for you. The National Center for Missing and Exploited Children (www.missingkids.com) is one of the largest champions of abducted children. They can also be reached at 1-800-THE LOST.

I hope if you are a recovering victim of parental abduction, that you have the resources for professional help. Having run into many walls, I know now the only way out of the darkness is with the help of a trained professional. I hope my story gives you hope for a joyous reunion and the confidence to continue your search for love and stability. There is light outside of the darkness, and it is warm.

No one understands the impact of parental abduction more than those who have experienced it. It is the same for those who have left the Watchtower and lost family and friends. There are many support groups for you if you have been disfellowshipped, and if you were abducted as a child. Some are listed at the end of this book.

If you are contemplating stealing your child from his or her mother or father, I pray you will be still for only a moment and realize the damage you will be heaping upon your beloved child, for it will affect your child's life permanently.

Every child deserves to know his or her own parents. We crave it and we need it. Do not deprive us of our own birthright. One day we will grow up, and see for ourselves the light of the truth.

Afterword

Margaret Burton Malone, Editor

Working as a volunteer at my son's school, I met a delightful lady, Nina, who became a great friend and later disclosed that she is a former Jehovah's Witness. She and many of her friends had been labeled "apostates" by the Watchtower, since they had turned away from their faith. As I grew closer to Nina and her family and was invited into their social circle, I saw extraordinary courage and strength in their resolution to have a "normal life" in spite of being spurned by Witness friends and family who followed their church's injunction to shun those who fell from their version of grace.

One evening, I dropped by Nina's home to collect my son after a play-date with her children. I was muddy and scruffy after a rainy afternoon cleaning my horse barn, and as I took off my boots to enter the living room, Nina introduced me to a couple I had never met before: Bryan McGlothin and his wife, Evelyne Tharet McGlothin. We shook hands and began to talk as if we'd been friends for years. Evelyne, being French, provided a welcome connection to Europe and we enjoyed talking about her country and my visits there, not to mention a few quips about silly European national rivalries.

Nina mentioned that I am a writer, whereupon Bryan began to tell me of his work on a book about his abduction. Looking back, it's an incongruous scene: a grubby, jeans-clad

210

Englishwoman sitting on her friend's immaculate floor, hugging the dog, chatting to an American actor and his French wife about parental abduction and religious fanaticism, while swigging good red wine.

Bryan's calm intensity told me he had something important to say. I was thrilled when he asked me to work with him on *Have You Seen My Mother*. Even though we had only discussed the book in the context of a jolly, spontaneous social gathering, Bryan's commitment, stamina, and clear moral compass stood out from the social niceties of the conversation. Later, when he sent me his first draft, I thoroughly enjoyed reading it and was honored to join him on a defining rite of passage for every writer: the crafting of a first book.

Have You Seen My Mother has social significance: a positive contribution to discourse about religion in our times. Those who turn from the Jehovah's Witnesses generally carry a heavy burden of regret and pain. Some seek escape from past trauma or emotional injury. Others desire opportunities typically denied to Witnesses: social connections, education, or the pursuit of wealth. They question the Witness faith and cannot reconcile their personal perspectives to it. They face a rough road into the world they have been taught to disregard. But those I know as apostates seem averse to self-pity: strong, wise people who think deeply about life and faith. They find great joy and satisfaction in experiences "worldly" people take for granted: decorating a Christmas tree, expressing a controversial opinion, voting, celebrating a child's birthday, even reading the Bible without the Watchtower's supervision. Bryan McGlothin's story contains each of these facets, set forth with the special power of an absorbing novel. I hope it helps people to think critically about religion and the choices people make in its name, regardless of faith or culture.

List of References

Page 85: Our Kingdom Ministry 2002 page 4, paragraph 9. Watchtower Bible and Tract Society, Inc. Brooklyn, NY

Page 88: Letter from Angie McGlothin, written on the road (New Mexico) to her parents, Bryan and Lola Mason (Baldwin Park, CA) written September 11th 1964. The letter was never mailed.

Page 88: Letter from Angie McGlothin (El Monte, CA) to my grandparents, Buck and Lucille (McLoud, OK), dated January 24th 1966. The letter to my grandparents would contained another letter from my mother to be forwarded to my father.

Page 89: Letter from Angie Stamper (El Monte, CA) to my father, via his parents (McLoud, OK) Written June 23th 1972.

Page 126: Letter written by my grandmother Lola Mae (Baldwin Park, CA), to her husband, Bryan (Merana, AZ). February 13th 1955.

Page 127: Letter written by my grandmother Lola Mae (Baldwin Park, CA), to her husband, Bryan (Merana, AZ). February 17th 1955.

Page 128: Letter written by my grandmother Lola Mae (Baldwin Park, CA), to my mother Angie Lenora McGlothin (McLoud, OK), on January 21st 1964.

Page 128: Letter written by my grandmother Lola Mae (Baldwin Park, CA), to my mother Angie Lenora McGlothin (McLoud, OK), on February, 5th 1964.

Page 129: Letter written by my grandmother Lola Mae (Baldwin Park, CA), to my mother Angie Lenora McGlothin (McLoud, OK), on March 19th 1964.

Page 129: Letter written by my aunt Sherry Irene Mason (Baldwin Park, CA), to my mother Angie Lenora McGlothin (McLoud, OK), on September 22nd

Page 150: Letter written by my grandmother Lola Mae (Baldwin Park, CA), to my mother Angie Lenora McGlothin (McLoud, OK), on January 13th 1964.

Page 151: Letter written by my grandmother Lola Mae (Baldwin Park, CA), to my mother Angie Lenora McGlothin (McLoud, OK), on March 8th 1964.

Page 151: Letter written by my grandmother Lola Mae (Baldwin Park, CA), to my mother Angie Lenora McGlothin (McLoud, OK), on November 12th 1963.

Page 151: Letter written by my grandmother Lola Mae (Baldwin Park, CA), to my mother Angie Lenora McGlothin (McLoud, OK), on January 21st 1964.

Page 152: Letter written by my mother Angie Lenora McGlothin (McLoud, OK), to her mother Lola Mae (Baldwin Park, CA), on May 11th.

Page 159: September 15th 1964, Freddie Lee McGlothin vs. Angie McGlothin. Petition for Separate Maintenance, District Court Pottawatomie County, State of Oklahoma No.10,786.

Page 159: December 31st 1964, Freddie Lee McGlothin vs. Angie Lenora McGlothin. Petition for Divorce, District Court Pottawatomie County, State of Oklahoma No.10,862.

Page 162: Letter written by my aunt Sherry Franco, now married (Covina, CA), to my mother Angie Lenora McGlothin (McLoud, OK), on February 14th 1965.

Page 172: Watchtower 1964 January 15 pp. 63-4 Questions from Readers, Watchtower Bible & Tract Society, Inc.

Page 173: March 1st 1965, State of Oklahoma vs. Freddie Lee McGlothin. Criminal Appearance Docket page 482, No. 9030.

Page 175: Letter from my father, Fred McGlothin (Louisville, KY), to Watchtower Bible and Tract Society, Inc. headquarters (Brooklyn, NY) March 13th 1967.

Page 182: Letter from the Watchtower Bible and Tract Society, Inc. (Brooklyn, NY) to my father, Fred McGlothin (Louisville, KY) March 15th 1967.

Page 183: April 3rd 1967, Freddie McGlothin vs. Angie McGlothin, Interlocutory Order Finding of Fact: Conclusions of Law: Decree, Jefferson Circuit Court, Chancery Branch, Forth Division, State of Kentucky, No.107 821.

Page 186: November 24th 1967, Angie Lenora McGlothin vs. Freddie Lee McGlothin, Buck McGlothin and Lucille McGlothin, Petition for Divorce, District Court of Oklahoma County, State of Oklahoma

No.139 574.

Page 188: April 3rd 1967, Freddie McGlothin vs. Angie McGlothin, Requisition for Copy Work, Jefferson Circuit Court, Chancery Branch, Forth Division, State of Kentucky, No.107 821.

Page 197: Cultic Studies Review Vol. 1, No. 2; International Cultic Studies Association (Formerly AFF, American Family Foundation)

Page 197: May 1st 1999 *Watchtower* magazine, Watchtower Bible & Tract Society, Inc.

Page 201: January 1st 1979 *Watchtower* magazine in "Questions from readers", Watchtower Bible & Tract Society, Inc.

Page 202: June 30th 2004, Letter from my daughter, Anna (East Texas), to me (Plano, TX) explaining she would no longer be speaking to me because I didn't hold the same doctrines as she.

Page 205: "Parental Child Abduction is Child Abuse" by Nancy Faulkner, Ph.D. Presented to the United Nations Convention on Child Rights in Special Session, June 9th 1999, on behalf of P.A.R.E.N.T. and victims of parental child abduction.

Helpful Resources

Recommended Reading

Father's Touch by Donald D'Haene
Crisis of Conscience by Raymond Franz
Jehovah's Witnesses and the Third Reich—Sectarian Politics Under Persecution by M. James Penton
In Search of Christian Freedom by Raymond Franz

Helpful Organizations

Take Root

P. O. Box 930,
Kalama, WA 98625
toll free: 1-800-ROOT-ORG
fax: (360) 673-3732
www.takeroot.org

National Center for Missing and Exploited Children

Charles B. Wang International Children's Building
699 Prince Street
Alexandria, VA 22314-3175
1-800-THE-LOST
www.missingkids.org/

National Clearinghouse on Child Abuse and Neglect Information

330 C Street, SW
Washington, DC 20447
Phone: (800) 394-3366 or (703) 385-7565
http://nccanch.acf.hhs.gov/

The Child Safety Institute (CAPS)

PO Box 176, Roslyn, NY 11576
516-621-0552
www.kidsafe-caps.org/

Adult Survivors of Child Abuse

The Morris Center
PO Box 14039,
San Francisco CA 94114-0039
415-452-1939
www.ascasupport.org/

Recommended Web Sites

Child sexual abuse within the Jehovah's Witnesses: http://silentlambs.org
Child abuse information: www.prevent-abuse-now.com/
Jehovah's Witnesses abuse survivor forum: www.lambsroar.org/
Promotes awareness of the Watchtower: www.freeminds.org
Unbelievable Watchtower Quotes: http://quotes.watchtower.ca/
Ex-Jehovah's Witness Forum: www.jehovahs-witness.com